Soul Trek
In the Universal Universe

Listening points to who you really are underneath all the things that continuously change

Eckhart

I am not what happened, I am the space in which everything happens that is my true identity.

Soul Trek
In the Universal Universe

by
JULIE GALE

Published by
Light Publishing

First published in 1996
by Light Publishing
The College of Psychic Studies
16 Queensberry Place
London, SW7 2EB

© 1966 Julie Gale

Made in the United Kingdom

ISBN 0 903336 26 X

The aim of LIGHT PUBLISHING and THE COLLEGE
OF PSYCHIC STUDIES is to explore all aspects of
spiritual and psychic knowledge.

The views expressed in all books published by LIGHT
PUBLISHING and THE COLLEGE OF PSYCHIC
STUDIES are those of the author, and do not necessarily
reflect the views of The College of Psychic Studies.

"We have room for all who realise the importance, in a
materialistic age, of expressing a belief that there is
something behind matter and that death does not end
all. . ." *From a preliminary meeting of the College, November
1883. This was the declared note of the then new College and
it remains so to this day.*

Typeset, printed and bound in Great Britain
by Whitstable Litho, Whitstable, Kent.

Contents

Introduction

In 1988 I sat down at my computer to write a novel, when I felt the presence of my beloved spiritual teacher, whom I had known for many years. He asked me if I would write a book for him and I heard him say some words that I began to type. I wrote for six months and here is an edited version of the result.

I did not continue to have things 'dictated to me' although I did occasionally hear a few words or even sentences. The material began to come in what I call 'thought bombs', complex ideas which I then had to disentangle and put into my own words. Hence a three-thousand-year-old spirit may use up-to-date wording. Sometimes he will insist on a particular way of saying something, and he is usually right.

I have written this book as if my teacher, the soul I call Alpha, was writing it. It is how I 'hear' it in my head, my mind. This sort of work is now called 'channelled material' and I am quite happy for it to be called that, but I prefer to say that it was received mediumistically by using my psychic senses. Either way, it does not matter. What is important is what it says! You may have difficulty in accepting that I converse with this ancient personage. Don't worry, so did I and I have been conversing with him for many years. I am the most sceptical of sceptics. You may think it mad, but then others say they contact energies, greater beings, space men and even God. To speak to the spirit of one who once lived on this earth seems quite reasonable.

Over the years I have had many instances of help, teaching, guidance, questions answered, forecasts coming true and even my life being saved. Most of all I have experienced 'love' of such a nature that it has changed my whole perception of life. I could only wish for everyone to be as lucky as I have been in their own spiritual searches. I hope that this book will help others to seek their own inner guidance and that I may read of their experiences in turn.

Julie Gale

Chapter 1

The Fire

There is a journey that every soul makes for the sake of love. An amazing journey which appears to take an eternity to complete. A journey that starts when the soul leaves the centre of all being – The Great Spirit – and ends with the return to its source. You, alive on earth – I, a soul who walked your earth several thousand years ago – everyone and everything are manifestations of these souls making this incredibly complex, and so important, round of existences in the Spiritual Universe. It is this Journey of the Soul that I wish to relate to you now.

What I am about to tell to you, through the earthly Medium taking down my thoughts, may seem strange and difficult to accept. Whether the information in this book is truth or untruth, real or false, does not matter. The important thing is that it makes you think. You may laugh it to scorn if you wish, or you may find that deep down, it was what you were beginning to think anyway. You could cast it aside for many reasons; for instance that you cannot feel I am what I say I am. Or it could be just the thing that sets you on a new and exciting path, the thing that gives meaning and reason to the life you lead in this modern world. I really don't mind what you choose to think about this book as long as I am given the chance, through this medium, to write it. If even one person is ever helped by it, it will be worthwhile. Who am I? I am Alpha, your esteemed servant, your mentor for the duration of your reading of these words, your representative of that state to which you definitely do not aspire. The dead! But oh, *SO ALIVE!* The name I have given is not my real one. My true identity while on your earth is not really important for I am only one of a group, a whole host of those who, like myself, according to you, are dead.

"Here we go," I hear you say, "It's going to be one of those sort of books, is it? How do we know you are who you say you are, what you say you are? The hand moving the pen or the fingers on the keyboard belong to a very 'live' human."

Right! But I no longer possess 'live' fingers and she does. If I want to tell you something, and I do, this is the only form of communication that I have in your world. Like it or lump it. *I* have to, and so does the Medium to whom the 'live' fingers belong. We use a mental link which she doubts herself, more often than not. It is not easy for any of us.

May I make a suggestion? Forget your misgivings for the time being and just suppose that you have a theory you are trying out, working on. Or suspend your disbelief temporarily and imagine, rather like reading a novel, that this situation, this form of communication does exist and is possible. When you have read my book or even as you are reading it, you can weigh up my words and consider if they mean anything to you. If they don't, fine, all well and good. What I say is not yet for you.

If I start a train of thought that interests you then I will be well pleased. I would not, even then, ask you to accept any part of what I say without consideration. Accepting what I say or who I say I am is not the important part. If the ideas sustain you in your journey through life, what does it matter where they come from: the human, physical mind that moves the pen, alive on your world – or minds that no longer inhabit worldly bodies? It is the ideas that matter, giving you food for thought, hopefully giving you a new perspective to life, to your life.

It is just one more way of looking at the meaning of existence and its mechanics but from what I consider is a much, much wider point of view.

I hope what you find here will light your way forward out of the long dark tunnel of dogmatic religions, any of them; shed more light on what they were about. You may like to use these ideas in conjunction with your own religion if you still cling to one; or if you find yourself without any religious beliefs, ideas or hopes, and yet are at a loss for guidance on the everlasting question, *Why am I here?* I hope some or any of my words will bring you comfort and an answer. Greetings to you, the seeker, you are taking steps along the road that can lead you back to where you rightfully belong: at one with the Spiritual Universe.

*   *   *   *   *

Let us make a start at what appears to you to be an end. The facts that I am about to lay before you do not constitute an entire picture of an ending of an earth plane existence by death. They are the simple rudiments. As yet the medical profession does not completely understand the workings of the body physical. How much more difficult to explain the body spiritual when so few of you can observe it, and those that do are disbelieved when they tell you what they can see. Nevertheless it is worth retelling the facts for they have been given to you many times before.

You, as you sit there, have two bodies. The one you can see, called a physical body, and one you cannot see, called an etheric body, sometimes also called the spiritual body. They are joined together by a cord of etheric tissue called the silver or etheric cord. It is similar to the baby-mother umbilical cord in that nutrients and other things pass through it, but dissimilar in other ways, for it stays in place during the entire physical life. When the two bodies separate and the cord breaks – *death ensues*. There we have it in a nutshell. Let us now take a closer look at the whole idea.

You now know that the physical world is made up of an uncountable number of atoms. Atoms are made up of a centre called a nucleus around which electrons revolve at speed. What you see as solid is an illusion. It is a constantly moving collection of atoms. These atoms can be broken down into particles and waves, which scientists are constantly discovering work in new and strange ways.

The etheric dimensions are made up from a substance which exists beyond any measurable range yet found by earthly scientists and is not really anything at all in your worldly sense of the word. Yet it is a basis of your physical world. It co-exists 'within' your atomic particles, and 'in between' your earthly atoms. There is also a difference in the speed-time dimension (or to be precise, there being 'no time') involved in co-existence with the physical universe, which I find too difficult to explain and is not necessary to your understanding of the above.

Might it be possible for earthly scientists to be able to find this etheric substance then? Yes it is, if they had the right instruments and looked at it with a different idea in mind than that which they think they should find. For although scientists have discovered much about the atom and its particles, they are still a long way from finding that which makes up the etheric dimensions and how it works. That is not to say they never will, for they are getting nearer to an understanding of atomic reality all the time.

The etheric body is then made up of what is a substance in the etheric sense of the word and therefore can exist in what appears to be the same portion of space as physical substance.

Why should this etheric body be, and which comes first, the etheric or the physical? I will tell you now. It is the etheric. Other things precede the etheric, but one thing at a time. I will say here and now though, the etheric body is NOT what is variously termed *The Mind*, *The Self*, *The Spark of Life*, *The Soul*. It is merely a transport, a housing of that essence, as is the physical body. As you exist and perceive in the physical body now, so you can exist in the etheric body. In fact, you are doing so now, at this very moment. It is not born when you die. It is in being right now and is the body that you will use after your physical life is over.

Let us consider what this duality means. The first fact is that you have a vehicle in which you can lead an afterlife. Not some odd, floating white balloon but a perfectly normal body. The second is that there is a place in which to lead that life which is just as normal to you as your present world.

Yes, a place, for not only is your body made up of this etheric substance, so are other objects which form a plane of existence around you. A place you can perceive. A place you can live, learn and love in, a home for your etheric body.

Now let me ask you this. Does nature on your world jump suddenly from one form to another? Does a caterpillar suddenly become a butterfly? Does the egg under the water suddenly become a dragonfly without progressing through the grub stages? Does a leaf fall to the ground and suddenly decay into mud? And does an embryo in the womb get itself born as a fully grown adult person? Is not the circle of life, death and decay slow and profound?

The natural law of slow change is not suddenly suspended at the death of a human. They do not immediately transform into some inconceivable being. No, it is rather a drift from one level to another which is your next door neighbour in the scale of life and creation.

The physical body can no longer be held together – it is decaying according to the law. It has co-existed with the etheric body which now takes its turn to house the essential particle which is you – your very essence. The etheric body sheds the physical body as some animals shed a dead skin. Your consciousness immediately looks out of etheric eyes, walks with etheric legs and breathes with etheric lungs. So little is different that you would not notice that anything had changed. The etheric cord gently breaks and is absorbed by the etheric body. And here you stand complete, a whole man or woman. But to the physical world you are truly dead. The physical body you leave behind is just that, no doubt at all. But you will be, and feel, more alive than you can ever remember.

*   *   *   *   *

Having discussed how one survives death it is only a step to considering dying not just once, but many times. For can you really learn all there is to know about life in your world in just one lifetime? Can you learn what it is like to be poor if you have riches all the way, or how a slave feels if you are always the master? What health, happiness is like when you have been locked in a useless body for fifty years? Can you know all about love when you have only been reviled and mistreated all your life? The answer to these and many other questions like them has to be '*no*'.

We do not expect you to assimilate this idea called reincarnation and begin to accept it straight away. But we would like you to take it on board as a supposition, a theory, because without it, nothing can follow. It is *THE KEY* to the whole of this book.

But what about all that dying and still living in a place that is just like home that I talked about previously? Where does that fit in with coming back here again and again?

That all happens, have no fear. It will happen at the end of your present life. But it is a very, very small part of the whole story. A story that I would now like to tell you of the journey of the soul. Any soul, your soul, my soul, all souls that have ever been or will be. Their journeys will not all be exactly the same, but the reason and the way they are undertaken is. So with the idea of rebirth salted away for later use I am going to introduce you to a completely different way of looking at what is generally called:

GOD AND CREATION.

You recall that I said the etheric was not that which is considered to be *The Flame of Life* or your very essence. There are many words for this certain something that humans have coined through the ages. It has never been found by man for it is beyond even the etheric which, as we discussed, has not yet been discovered. For the etheric substance is by no means the end of the story. There are many further layers of existence which lie behind the etheric on finer and faster dimensions. If they were stripped away, one would eventually arrive at the level of the Flame of Life. I now want to tell you how it came to be there and how it makes you the beginning and end of everything.

To do this I am going to take you from the point of your existence to a place far beyond human or etheric experience or understanding. I refer to that estate to which we all aspire, yearn for, even when we don't know that is what we are doing, a place where one would be in *Communion with 'The Great Spirit'*. It is not that it is an impossible thing to do from the body in which you now reside, but it is somewhat difficult.

Try to put yourself in the position of attempting to explain to a being from another planet who has never been to your world what it is like. This being has never seen a tree because his world is a desert. You are on his spaceship as a visitor and he can translate your language through some kind of gizmo he has about him. Imagine trying to convey to him the idea of a tree in words. If you could then ask him to draw a picture of what you had explained to him you would probably be quite shocked at your inability to pass over an accurate description. It would not be your fault because he has no experience on which to base his conception. Now, if he showed you pictures of his world and you picked out something like a tree and said it was like the tree you had tried to explain to him but yours was larger and had green bits all over it, he may begin to get a better idea. But suppose green was not a colour of his spectrum, you would find yourself back in difficulties again.

How much more difficult if the idea is purely a conception of the mind, a philosophy or theological idea. Or if it were formed of anything that could only be described as *power, energy or thought*. I'll tell you what would happen. You would have to resort to symbols and stories to illustrate your point.

What I hope will be different in this communication is this. After giving you a symbol I will try to explain it as far as I can in modern terms. Terms that I feel you, and particularly those about to be born, will readily understand because of the greater quality of your intelligence. Let us make a start. I am going to give you a symbol and it is this:

Let us take a fire, the very heart of a fire, the centre, where the heat is so intense that it burns white and you can hardly bear to look at it for fear your eyes will be burnt out, even at a distance. Surrounding this core of white heat, in circles of decreasing intensity, there is fuel blazing from shades of yellow to orange red, flames that appear to dance with joy in their existence. Overhead sparks of blue and green snap and leap into the air, turning to carbon but still glowing with the heat.

Fuel is piled on the fire waiting to fall towards that blazing heart, and round about lie piles of logs waiting for their turn to join the conflagration, the glory of the flames. The fire is in a clearing of a forest and trees, large and small, grow in profusion.

As the sparks shoot skyward, they shine with the brightness of that inner heart of the fire, then drift away, cooling. They later fall to the floor of the forest where the trees take them up as nutrients. They pass back and forth to the ground many times, becoming leaves, flowers and fruits. Later they become the very wood of which a tree is composed whose time has come to be felled and stored ready for the fire. In that form, they move ever nearer the time they will be placed on the fire, there to crackle and dry before bursting forth with renewed energy, giving their all for the whole and yet being a part of that whole. They pass through the flames, the red and yellow heat, and finally, yet again, become a part of that fantastic power that is the centre of the fire.

That is the picture I want you to hold in your mind while I refer to the various parts that go to make it complete. Symbolically we have all the essential tokens to represent what I will call throughout this book the *'SPIRITUAL UNIVERSE'*. What do I mean by that term? Well all that goes to make up every universe there ever was, is or will be. Not only the one you can see, or the ones you will pass to upon your death. I also speak of that from which this and other universes make their appearance. Let me explain my symbol furthersource of all being which some term God. As you will have noticed I call It *'The Great Spirit'* and shall do so throughout this book. As I sense neither wholly male or female principle in this power I shall not stay with convention and call The Great Spirit He but shall use It. In the English language 'It' is inanimate but the Great Spirit is anything but that. It is life itself.

The Great Spirit then is the fire of love, the total source of power of the Spiritual Universe. It is all being, happiness and joy, total bliss, ecstasy and love. It is what makes and renews the whole of creation and lights it to its uttermost ends.

But all powers need fuel. It is one of the immutable laws. So the fire casts out particles of itself to be what one might term sacrifices to the future continuation of the central fire. These particles go with joy and happiness, knowing they are to be of service to the wondrous heart of which they also know they are a part. They are pure and have a centre and more still glowing with the power of their source. These particles represent the soul and its first steps on its migration, its round of eternity. The Great Spirit has sacrificed some particles of Itself and caused them to start a separate round of existence.

Here there is a point I must make. Our symbol does not work in one respect because the spark in the centre of a piece of flying material goes out. But the flame of life, that radiant energy of a soul, *NEVER GOES OUT.* It is there forever.

The spark of material rises into the air and drifts to some part of the forest. This is likened to the existences of the soul while still within the sight of the Great Spirit, existences composed of varying forms and lives and experiences of all types.

There comes a time when the particle must come to rest on the forest floor. The descent from the air represents many existences drawing etheric particles to its energy centre. When the particle lands on the forest floor it represents the time of taking strong inorganic and organic forms of existence. The many particles rise and fall into the trees to become leaves, representing flowers and fruits, animal lives, or lives as humans. This will be explained more fully later.

As consummate knowledge allows cessation of these cycles, the particle becomes an actual part of one of the trees proper and represents the post-etheric lives where further progress is made towards its destiny by refining itself, losing its dross, all that is unnecessary. The particle then represents the completed soul as it draws ever closer to the fire, knowing it has brought with it that *FUEL* which is needed by the Great Heart of the fire. Eventually the particle can rejoice in its return and in once more being a part of that Great Heart.

There is your symbol. A fire burning in a forest. Do not think that the Great Spirit is composed of fire. It is but a symbol of the love-power that *It* is. It is the nearest I can come to explaining that power in simple terms. Fire is often greatly feared in your world. In this sense, it merely represents a source of power.

First let us discuss the Great Spirit and all things will follow. I am not going to argue with you whether It does or does not exist, but tell you what I find to be so. It is up to every single individual soul to come to his, her or its own recognition of the Great Spirit. I can only act as a signpost.

The Great Spirit is all pervasive. It is in everything, of everything, and is everything. You and I have our being in It. It is the master mind of all master minds and within It reside all the rules and laws of creation. It is the physicist, the scientist, the philosopher, the mathematician and logician, It is the poet, the artist, the writer, the musician, the inspirer of the Spiritual Universe. It is that which knows every molecule and atom of matter and anti-matter and that which is neither; every pulse and rhythm of energy that ever was, is, or will be. It is every emotion from hate to love. Say that and we have still said nothing of what the Great Spirit is. And we have a particle of this great wonder within every one of us! How can this be?

Creation is one of the great mysteries of your universe. Did it start all at one moment or is it continuous, never having a beginning or an end?

In the light of my own studies since death, I plump for the latter. Beginnings and endings pertain very much to your physical world; they are an illusion but that is another matter. A story of how the world was created is part of most creeds and sects, from the 'Let there be light' of the Bible to the 'Dream time' of the Australian Aboriginal.

These stories were given as symbols to man at certain stages of his history, much as I have given you the symbol of the fire in the forest. But they were not told that it was a symbol as you have been told. You are educated to modern standards and know what your scientists propound about the formation of the world and the aeons of time taken before it was in a state suitable for life.

Whatever, this great mind-love-power Spirit is the centre of all being. It is beyond nearly every being separated from It to understand the nature of this mind-love-power except at one certain moment in its circle of eternity. I therefore feel it does not serve us to speculate on the Great Spirit's nature, only to accept that part of It which we know to be true.

What is that? It is the one truth you know is certain as you read these words. Here and now you can say '*I EXIST*'. You are. You are in being. You do not know where you have been or where you are going but you can state with certainty *You Exist!* That feeling, that certain knowledge, is the spark of the Great Spirit you carry within you, and through that spark you can recognise, should you choose, the truth of the Great Spirit. It may not be now or in the near future or even in this lifetime, but one day you will know and understand that the Great Spirit is you and you are a part of the Great Spirit. All that you see and all whom you see join in this vast creation to make up the one supreme being.

The Great Spirit, knowing all things, has to look to the continuation of Its being. Much the same thing happens to your own body where new cells are continually being created to replace the old. I have stated that all powers need fuel, as the fire did in our symbol. The Great Spirit is not outside this law. Indeed, it is that law. It appears that what happens is that It parts with some of Its inner self and separates it from Its central being, as the fire casts away its sparks. It sends the particles away with their permission, for they are portions of Itself. Then they pass through many changes until they are in a form that can be re-assimilated and renew the power of creation. Did you ever run across the symbol of the snake eating its own tail? It is a very old symbol which is meant to represent this very thing we are discussing. It is an excellent example of a good symbol. Nothing could say it better. Eternity is, as you say these days, ongoing. It feeds on itself. From the moment the particles of The Great Spirit are sent out to their return is our story. Yours and mine, everyone's. For what I am going to term your 'soul' was formed out of, is one of, those very particles. Not the individual form recognised as you today, or what you will be tomorrow, but nevertheless you. The 'I Exist' you can proclaim with certainty.

This has been a lot to take in and as yet so little has been explained as to how it happens. What I have tried to do from the outset is give you a fact to chew on. A possible answer as to why we are on this journey of life. We are gone to fetch the fuel without which everything would blink out of existence. What that fuel is and how we come by it is a discussion for a future chapter. Meanwhile take courage from the idea that there is a reason to our lives.

Chapter 2

The Angelic Realms

How could you ever leave perfection? How could you pass up eternal bliss, true Nirvana, to go to imperfection and worse? Why? The answer to all these questions is *LOVE*.

Love and love alone is the cause behind everything the Great Spirit is and does. It is truly a force with which to be reckoned. A real power. It is an absolute and its strength can be tested any time you like. It can save and it can kill. It can console and it can smother. It can build and it can destroy.

There is one other thing that you might like to think about. Like the Great Spirit, love is invisible. How often we say, one to another 'God is Love'. Yes, the Great Spirit is as invisible to me as It is to you. It does not mean that you or I cannot sense the Great Spirit or experience It. It does not mean that you or I will never see It.

I would like to draw on our symbol of the fire once more to point out the way that the fire pours forth sparks, particles of itself, in a continuous, unceasing manner, not just one burst and finish. Sometimes it may explode with energy and pour forth showers of particles in what seems an excess and at other times there is a steady, but slower flow. There are also times of relative quiet with only a small number of motes leaving the source.

In other words the Great Spirit parts with some of Itself in a great continuous flow, asking It to go forth and experience. See – feel – hear – touch – and most of all *BE*. It is as if It is asking mind to actualise and become body.

Now to ask me to remember what happened at this point is no better than asking yourself. You cannot even remember before your birth, or even your birth and a few years after. Even I don't recall it precisely but I do have a feeling about it and a remembered yearning. Rather like some folk on your earth have a vague remembered feeling about a previous life on earth.

How do I know about these things? Just as you are about to learn, I have been taught. I have discovered about the peregrinations of the soul by being tutored on the subject since my last earthly death. It might interest you to know that it was not thought a good thing by all on my side of death that the information in this book be given at all. However, it was decided that it was worth trying.

When the particles which I shall call 'Total Souls' first leave the Great Spirit they drift and dream for a long time. In fact there is no conception of time for there is none as such. They still have their being in that pure mind-love-power. They are unsullied, rarefied and beautiful. They are so much in communication with their source that it is almost as if they had not left. But they have. They have become part of the Pre-Angelic Hosts. They are about to experience the Pre-Angelic Realms. Did you ever wonder from where those stories of floating around and gazing on the Godhead stem? I think it is from this period, for it seems that is what happens in these realms. It is almost impossible to know and only a few do. For how can any of us be in such a pure state that we can go there and find out?

Gradually, gently, the total souls begin to move towards a point of choice, a mental choice, for they are composed of all that is of the mind. This choice is for ever, or at least for their round of eternity.

At this time the total souls are the mind-love-power that is their source and are in a state of joy. But they do feel their separation keenly. This feeling is the catalyst of the choice. It is the beginning of the double paradox that is the Great Spirit. The Positive and Negative. The Yin and Yang. The Good and the Bad. The Right and Left-hand paths. The two sides of everything in creation.

The total souls seem to form into two distinct groups or, to put it another way, they choose one path or the other. The two groups stay intermixed at this point and it would be difficult to differentiate between each of them. They continue to mill about the realms near the Great Spirit. It does not seem to make one whit of difference to their communion with the Great Spirit. It continues to know and love them all equally and without exception, something It goes on doing for ever. The law of gradual change has been subtly operating, and imperceptibly these total souls are drawn towards their destiny.

Before we discuss that destiny let us look at some other points about these wondrous total souls. For they are wondrous. They are not childlike. They are straight from the Godhead, the source. They are the Great Spirit separated from Itself. The vast masses of these total souls are not yet the individual souls they will later become, they are Group Souls. Yes, as cells form together to make a whole, what might be termed soul-cells group together to make one of these wonderful beings. Like all paradoxes there is the occasional exception which I will go into later.

Where are you then? You are, or were, one of those soul-cells, or more likely, were a part of one of those soul-cells. Perhaps that fact might help you to understand why we do not remember that time except as a feeling deep inside. From that point we have such a long, long way to go.

On the other hand if it makes you feel small and insignificant I am afraid there is nothing I can do about it, for the truth is we, you and I, at that point of our existence, were insignificant. But also indispensable. For the part is loved as much as the whole. And you were the whole point to it happening anyway, you and me and those uncountable other parts of soul-cells.

These beings have their existence in a form so removed from anything we know that the nearest we can come to explaining it is Mind. Where they are geographically in the Spiritual Universe is not known either but the answer appears to be 'everywhere'. They interpenetrate everything and are the basic mind-love-power of the Spiritual Universe. They are the mind-love-power net within which you have your being. They are the nearest contact to the Great Spirit. When you address the Great Spirit, it is through them that your 'Prayer' passes. We shall have more to say on the subject of prayer but here we mean the cry of a soul to the Great Spirit for guidance, help, consolation or thanks.

It is as if the purpose of these beings is to enable the central being of the Great Spirit to have contact with all the parts of Itself. It may be possible that one of these fantastic beings can contact us. I have experienced beings that I just could not understand except for the great love that came from them. I do not think they appear in any form either to you on the physical earth or us in the etheric and beyond. But they are Mind, so maybe they can impinge on our minds and cause us to 'see' them in a form suitable to our needs. I do not think this happens very often because the Great Spirit has so many other avenues of contact which are nearer to our level of development. You see, the highest, most magnificent, ultra being that you can imagine is still not what these Pre-Angelic beings are. I have not really been able to explain the Great Spirit as I would like. These souls are no different from It except that there is a separation from their source. They have not changed – yet.

Eternity is not a word that signifies anything in the length of time these Pre-Angels stay in this form. Somewhere, somehow, the very reason for their separation from the Great Spirit draws them inexorably towards making the peregrination that is essential. The journey they have undertaken. The sacrifice they have said they would make. At this point they do not seem able to return to their source although I am not saying this is not possible, should a soul change its mind. It just does not seem possible, with the knowledge of the Great Spirit that they have and the love of which they are composed, that they would not go through with their intended purpose. They know the continuation of the Spiritual Universe depends on them.

Like the spark from our fire symbol, cooling a little after leaving the fire and its outer layer turning to carbon, the Pre-Angels become, little by little, more separated from their source. They gather to themselves more of what might be called energy particles which in turn makes them cloak down, change, so they are no longer identical to the Great Spirit. This cloaking down is a process started in these rarefied realms and is a principle that we shall come to know very well.

Their decision to allow this cloaking down happens when the realisation comes that only by undertaking the awesome journey of the soul can they ever be where they truly want to be: at one with the heart of the universe, once again a part of the Great Spirit. With this yearning being the one and only disturbance to their consciousness, they begin to express themselves more strongly in the Angelic or Energy Realms.

The Angelic realms are what might be termed the Anteroom to the presence of the Great Spirit. They are so near to Its being that they are absolutely pervaded by Its presence. There is still a drifting, dreaming quality to these realms but each total soul has more self-actuality, a presence of its own. It can have an experience of its own, choose a form of existence for longer or shorter periods.

The total souls still interpenetrate everything but are now able to actually be in one place or another rather than everywhere. But more, they are the basic 'Energy' network of creation and that is their part, their place in the scheme of creation.

It is a period for the total souls to begin to express themselves by having what I can only call 'lives'. It bears no resemblance to a life in our terms but there is no other word to use that expresses it as well. The total souls have a series of existences in the sphere to which they pertain. They are gentle, peaceful times, lovely and innocent, always within the contact of the Great Spirit.

Here a definite form to what might be termed the character of each total soul begins. The part of creation to which they are going to attach themselves is chosen, for there are many.

You will recall I said in the Pre-Angelic realms, the total souls made a choice, a choice of positive or negative. Here in these realms this choice becomes more evident. It has a direct influence upon all the other decisions that the total soul makes. It colours them.

These lovely beings always have help and guidance either from the source itself or from other total souls of greater experience. They also have what your world calls 'Free Will'. They are never forced into being or doing anything that is not of their choosing.

That the total souls need guidance may seem odd, for you would think that they were all-knowing being straight from the source. But this is not so and I will have to explain their composition a little more closely for you to understand.

Not only does the Great Spirit continuously pour forth Itself but the particles so sent vary in kind as the sparks from the fire might differ in size and colour, strength and brightness, shape and content.

As I have mentioned they are mostly group souls, that is they are formed of soul-cells. Occasionally there is a total soul that is so self-contained that it comes forth alone. It is very, very rare and comes always for a special purpose. This total soul will have come and gone on the journey of the soul uncountable times and it could be said was God incarnate in the Spiritual Universe. It is a total soul of unimaginable magnitude and abilities. It is very different from the total souls we have been discussing, yet it is as subject to the laws of the universe as any other total soul. It will experience all that the humblest total soul will experience.

For at the opposite end of the scale there are very new, humble souls who have never made the journey before, literally newly created. There are also many, many types of soul between the two extremes. These are all group souls but they vary in that they may have had many cycles of existence or only a few.

Here we have an important fact. The number of souls of which they are comprised seems to be smaller the more journeys they have made, and greater the less times they have been out from their source. The only explanation I have ever found for this is that perhaps – perhaps – each soul-cell in the older total soul is already comprised of many souls that will never separate again. This may be the answer to the single total soul, perhaps it is comprised of many souls, fused to become as one.

To return to the Angels and their experiences, perhaps you can now see that there are those about them who, having more knowledge and wisdom within them, can guide the more lowly. Do not think that by lowly they are any the less. In fact in some ways they are more nearly the Great Spirit because of their innocence and naïveté. Delightful young souls.

After a time there is a drifting away of these souls as they seek experiences of a less refined nature. More particles of energy are pulled to them and eventually something new happens. They attract, or are attracted to, something that is a cross between energy and etheric matter. For the first time they make contact with the universe of their choice rather than wander the Spiritual Universe. Do not think that this will limit them for the choices within any one universe are more than the stars you see in your night sky. There is, though, a certain tenor to each universe and it has something to offer in the way of life and life forms that will be different from every other.

They could choose from many universes, all existing at the same time as yours, each with systems and worlds without number. They provide for every avenue of life form, some similar to your own and some inexplicably different. The others do not matter to us for we will never touch upon them. Ours is what I will call the Etheric/Physical Universe and is just one of the universes within the Spiritual Universe. It is the one where we have our being, where we journey at this point in our journey of the soul.

All these universes, plus the energy and mind realms, make up one whole Spiritual Universe. Each one balances against another to create a complete pattern. We may have lived in one of those other universes while on another cycle of eternity, I do not know, nor do I think it matters. They exist, that's all.

The Angel soul becomes attached to one of these universes and draws particles of its make-up to itself. It does this by personifying itself in its first series of existences that are not wholly of the energy principle. I think these existences are more of an observing, watching and contemplative nature. It is of a very tentative construction and easily terminated. A flirting with the grosser particles, each time returning to the lower Angelic realms. But some etheric particles entwine with the being's essential self and gradually it becomes more involved.

This goes on happening until the 'weight' of grosser particles that have become a part of the total soul cause the next stage in its existence. The movement towards this change is noticeably faster in those that have made the negative choice but in the end all move towards it. It is called the downward spiral because the total soul plunges further and further into etheric-energy matter. It is, of course, neither downward, upward nor sideways, but something that happens to the soul.

You know how, in your own existence, if someone holds a resentment close for many years about something that happened in their childhood, they can go on in their lives to rebel and generally cause woe and anguish throughout their adult lives. They also seem only able to see the selfish view point and will often go to great lengths to gratify their needs and desires. Now that is taking the worst possible negative trait of personality that could be encountered. Some are able to control these feelings to a point that only a few come through, even turn it to advantage and good for others. Negative is just as strong as positive. Think about it.

It is the same with the negative Angelic ones. They seem to fall towards these kinds of reactive emotions. Not only do they fall away and become enmeshed in grosser particles quicker, they choose rather negative forms in which to have their being.

Why does the Great Spirit allow souls to become negative, drift towards paths that do seem to lead to trouble? I can only make a suggestion that was given me by one of my teachers. Could it be that all creation must conform to the positive-negative relationship that seems to exist through all things? Must It allow this to happen to be able to continue in existence Itself? I really cannot tell you for sure. That these positive and negative principles exist we all know and later in the book we will follow this divergence more closely.

This downwards spiral did not happen just once but has always been happening and is still happening, will continue to happen. I want you to get a sense of this continuousness in the universe. Let me put it another way.

You talk about generations, as if they happened say, every thirty years. Right on a certain date, the next generation is born? At the end of the line, the last die! Of course not. It is all going on at the same time, births, deaths, lives. One generation merges with another. So it is with all the Spiritual Universe. Everything is always happening somewhere, to someone or something. So it is with the Angels. In their realms you would find these total souls at all stages of involvement with the etheric-energy particles.

There comes a moment when the total soul crosses a divide, a point where it can no longer live in the Angelic realms. It has become a being on the highest level of the Etheric/Physical Universe. Now something very new and different starts to take place. The total soul can no longer hold together as one, the etheric particles begin to loosen the soul-cells of which it is comprised and break apart.

Now that might sound rather painful and unpleasant. It is not, it is only natural. Does not everything in your world break down into its constituent parts? That is all that is happening to the total soul. The first break down into parts. A breakdown that is to continue happening is the whole purpose of the journey. The method by which its purpose is fulfilled.

The total soul turns inward and almost gives birth to the soul-cells. Consciousness is passed out; from now on it is shared by the individual soul-cells. There is a remaining network of energy and mind that joins these soul-cells and makes them recognise themselves in each other. But the concept of total consciousness is now over. All that has been experienced is passed to the parts. Each then takes responsibility for its portion of the whole.

In the older total soul these soul-cells will remain as a total soul and not separate. But as I have stated before, they may consist of fused souls and therefore only appear as one. Any total soul below this highest level always breaks at this time into its constituent soul-cells, each of which becomes a smaller version of the Angelic being they made up.

It is not difficult to see that when this break up of the Angelic form takes place the parts are no longer capable of close communion with the Great Spirit. It is a communion that has been growing less and less but was still there, providing guidance, but now it is no longer recognised so easily. The thoughts of these soul-cells are towards the fine etheric worlds among which they find themselves. That is as it should be. Each period of the journey has its purposes and rightness. They are eager for experience and that experience is forthcoming in a richness that has to be seen to be understood and believed.

It may not seem that giving you this information about the Pre-Angelic and Angelic realms could mean a lot to you. It is all in the past. Quite so, but you learn the history of your nation and your world when at school. This is the history of your Spiritual Universe. There is one great difference. You may not have experienced every period of history (if you did you probably don't remember it) but you did experience what I have told you about, you were a part of just such a being for aeons and aeons, time out of mind, so long ago that there are no words to express it. It is your history and mine. It is in our history that we will find ourselves, understand our present selves. I personally find the Angelic realms most interesting for they are outside our physical branch of creation, outside the etheric and so different.

Chapter 3

Nearer To Home

This book is not intended as a new scripture that must be believed or revered. It is information to help you understand the complexities of the universe. It is history in the sense that it happened to us, you and me. It is current affairs in the sense that it is still happening, right now!

As the soul-cells plunge into the etheric, which is the material of their new make-up, they begin to draw existences to themselves, each one of a denser nature than the last. Every time an existence finishes, a few of the etheric particles the soul-cell has just experienced will remain in its make-up. In time there is a shell of these differing levels of etheric substance personifying on the scale at which the soul-cell is cognisant, probably visible to those who are on the same wavelength.

It is difficult to understand the composition of these 'shells' and what they would look like if we could see them. One thing that these early existences would not look like is 'human', particularly the shell in the early post-Angelic state which is very tentative, barely in existence.

Let us look back a moment. We have the pure centre, which is of the Great Spirit, which first draws a web of energy to itself, a basic power house. During the fall the energy so drawn becomes of a coarser nature until it attracts the etheric-energy particles. I have called them this for they are a cross between the two and difficult to describe any other way. They are one step down from pure energy. Then on down through the etheric experiences. Can you see the build up of what might be called concentric, yet interpenetrating, forms to hold that central essential essence that is the Great Spirit? Something of each experience is left with the soul and creates the repository to which the next particles will be drawn.

This would seem to say that these beings almost experienced lives and deaths and so they have in a way. But it is more a drifting at will, in and out of substances of a new nature to them. They go into them when they want to and come out likewise. They can create a form or take on an existing type of form as they wish. There are many planes of existence in which they can experiment and enjoy their freedom.

At first the total group of soul-cells will have experiences together but as the particles they attract grow coarser, heavier, they become more separated, turn inwards upon themselves and develop independently. This is the whole purpose of this period – the ripening of the soul-cells, getting ready for their next stage of existence.

I am sure you can see the pattern forming by now. The very gradual drawing of energy and substances to the soul centre, creating the housing of that which is the Great

Spirit. There is a law here that continues for a long time. At each stage, as I have said, the soul retains a certain amount of the particles of the last 'life'. From then on it can only draw particles of a like or coarser nature to itself. It cannot refine itself, pass backwards through the realms of which it had previously been a part. It is this law that persuades the soul to go forward on its journey at all stages until a certain point.

As the total soul loosens its hold, the central mind-love-power that is a part of the Great Spirit continues to reside within each and every one of the soul-cells. Because it is the Great Spirit, no part is any less than the whole and never loses touch with the Great Spirit, although the soul-cell is not conscious of that fact. That is, most soul-cells are not. The older the soul is, the more it remains in contact, able to receive guidance and succour from its very source. Even when the older total soul comes to this breakdown into constituent soul-cells, these soul-cells are still more conscious of the Great Spirit. The younger the soul the quicker it loses sight of its origin.

What is the purpose of this breaking apart, breaking down? It is a fission that releases energy and creates form, just as you break down your atoms for power. It also releases the soul-cell to individual experiences. No one cell will have quite the same thing happen to it as another, so it increases the experience possibilities of the whole.

Remember that the single, very experienced older soul does not break apart at this stage, but goes into the experiences that are about to happen still intact. These souls are very rare and are on the journey for a very special purpose which I will explain in due course. The total souls that are not quite so experienced still break into soul-cells at this point.

Why is all this experience needed? The obvious answer is to gain knowledge. Yet that is not an answer in itself, is it? Gaining useless trivia. Actually the knowledge is on different levels. One is experiential intelligence. The other is learning to manipulate, to control the surrounding dimension in which a total soul and later the soul-cell is operating. Learning the chemistry, physics and wavelength of each and every type of existence is essential as you will see. We have called it a journey but it is in reality a progress from one form to another with a purpose at each stage. But I must not jump ahead.

Now you may feel that just gathering knowledge is something that is a not a purpose in itself. Gained knowledge necessitates that it be used at some point. This is true but I think this accumulation of knowledge and wisdom is the basket in which we carry the fuel we have set out to gather, that which we have set out to find on this pilgrimage of the spheres.

There is not much more I can tell you about the upper regions of the etheric existences except to say that gradually they become totally etheric with the previous layers still there, but not apparent. When this has happened the soul-cells are very much on their own and go about their own business; they have purpose and things to do and be. A usefulness that is in preparation for the next stage.

It is said and thought of this and following stages of existence that these beings have no soul, that they are soulless, merely elementals. This is not true! They are souls at a certain stage in their existence. Their soul is no different from your own and for a while in the higher etheric regions they are more conscious of it than many of you physical humans.

The reason why they are thought to be elementals is because the existences they go through are often of the nature of being something rather than someone. At first they are souls of constituent parts of the etheric worlds they inhabit, the equivalent of minerals, plant life and so on of your world. Later they can take existences of fabulous animals in strange worlds. Always each incarnation is denser than the last until they begin to get the feeling of connection with solid form. Not as you experience it, but more than they have known before.

Here the weight of the etheric particles again causes a change in the soul-cell's make-up. The soul-cell itself begins to break down into its individual parts, individual souls. Still they will hold together for a long, long time. Eventually the break up will happen but before that is possible there comes a long drawn out incarnation as the soul-cells now draw the first physical particles to themselves.

This will not be directly as a human nor yet even as an animal, for there is so much to learn before that can happen. Physical matter is a very different proposition from anything in which the soul has previously survived. Why? Many reasons, but most of all it is not malleable to thought in quite the same way as previously experienced, something we have not talked about as yet, just a mention of taking forms and holding them by will-power. Remember in all the previous spheres the beings have been mind, energy, then etheric in constitution. This has meant that all the particles with which they have so far been in contact, the equivalent of atoms, molecules, can be drawn to them by thought and placed wherever they desire. If the idea that thought can affect substance, whatever its composition, seems impossible, that is because you have now entered a sphere that is impervious to thought except on a very basic level.

Thought seems to be unreality to you for although you experience it every waking moment of your life, and one could say in sleep as well, it never appears to directly affect your surroundings. You have to put out your hand to move something or make an object. You have to move your mouth and breathe out air in certain patterns to convey your thoughts to one another. The thought cannot pass directly from person to person. I think you feel you ought to be able to send your thoughts out or make them felt by the atoms of your world. That is because of the aeons of time you were able to do just that to your surroundings.

In fact, right to the bottom levels of the etheric pre-physical worlds you were able to take on a form by just wanting to be that form. You also had to continue to hold that form during its existence by effort of will, yes, the whole complex form. In the physical, the soul has to know how to control the basic elements, to coerce the atoms to make the form it requires. Once that has happened the form will hang together on its own without too much conscious effort by the soul, only a certain amount of direction. This iron grip of the physical is what is sought. It leaves more mental capacity free for other things. It also allows time to examine other things held in a continuous shape and form.

Now as the soul-cells grow heavy and begin the last break up into their constituent parts, the physical beckons. But they cannot use the old methods of getting themselves into these regions, the physical, by which I mean all the worlds that operate on your wavelength. Your world and all those countless stars, planets, galaxies that you can see and millions more beyond the reach of human vision. The newly loosened soul particles, which I will call 'souls', have to find a different way to express themselves. They have to learn a whole new method of gathering and attaching themselves to the particles of physical matter. This is done by starting at the very bottom of the scale of existences in the physical sphere and incarnating in the lowest form possible. That is the mineral.

"MINERAL!" I hear you shout. *"ME A STONE?"*

Yes, you a stone, a rock, an ore, a jewel, water, light, a spirit of the air. Yes indeed.

You will recall what I have said about these souls being thought elementals. This then is their form on your very world and accounts for early man's ideas of non-souls, gods, dead humans, living within the local rocks or stones erected to be worshipped, and later the idea came about that these elementals could be harnessed by magic forces and incantations. None of which was ever true. The souls incarnating within minerals are almost totally unaware of other forms of existence, even when directly disturbed. You see, they are in a dreaming state. A just 'being' state. And it lasts for a very, very long time.

How long ago since your world spun off in an explosion and cooled to be the planet you live on? Well, the souls that attached themselves at that time are still present and will be till your planet, your universe no longer exists! It is their experience of mineral. Not one soul really, trillions. Some will be grouped as one type of mineral and they will all be constituent parts of the same soul-cell.

Even the older souls have to pass through this type of incarnation, for without it they just cannot progress to the next stage. However, the greatest of total souls will still remain one, as will other souls of lesser but still a very high nature. They remain a soul-cell for the next stages. Both these types of souls are so rare as to seem almost non-existent but they must be mentioned for they are an important part of the whole.

Within the etheric there are thousands of similar physical universes that are there now, have been, or are about to appear. Each one will have its quota of souls incarnating as the minerals in that universe, all held there for the duration of its existence. It may seem to be an extraordinary length of time for one incarnation, but recall – the soul has been on much longer sojourns in other forms and has already had a time of being as an etheric mineral. It does not seem long to the soul.

That there are other worlds may be hard enough to take in, let alone other universes, but do not be small-minded. Your world, your physical universe, is not, repeat not, the only one that can have, will have, a so-called 'life form' living on it. Those souls at this time incarnating as the minerals of your very home will have their turn on similar planets to yours in other universes that will be there when they need them. You had your being as mineral on a world, in a galaxy, a universe, that no longer exists. If it did, you would still be there! Are you getting some conception of the time and scope there is within the Great Spirit? Forgive me for hammering it home. The Great Spirit is limitless and what we are discussing is the limitless material that somehow It provides, or allows us to use for the intended purpose of the soul gaining experience.

At this stage, then, we coerce the particles of physical materials to form into atoms and thence into molecules. As you can imagine, it is done by thousands of souls joining together. They are helped by the older souls and over-seen by the Great Spirit. I sometimes feel as if this material that we live within is the body of the Great Spirit. It allows us to use the material as we wish. It has to do this in order to let us fulfil our purpose, which is really Its purpose. Yet we are the Great Spirit so the purpose is the same.

I am sure you can see that this brings up the problem of understanding what you call 'Creation'. Well, it is an ongoing thing like everything else. Worlds, universes being formed or blinking out of existence, it's happening all the time. As regards the souls that animate any particular formation, one might wonder what happens when some larger formation explodes and creates several suns, worlds, planets, moons, dust. I am told that the explosion is the end of one set of souls' incarnation and the beginning of the next. When a star goes into nova, it probably has a change of soul. I don't know for sure but there is a reconstitution of its materials so it appears probable. Yes, there are always enough souls wanting to use any material that is free for use. Loose material is never a problem. It is often souls looking for material rather than material going spare.

Why do they want to use these materials to form elements of such a strong grip, to fix themselves to something that appears to be so inanimate? It is the soul units of the soul-cells fighting to have their separate existence. When it is over they will have their first totally separate existence. It is not known whether the souls take more than one incarnation as mineral. It could be. It seems that they do move from one form to another while their universe is in existence. That is, as the elements are used by outside forces the soul has to realign itself. This is obvious if you consider say lava, heated and flowing then congealing into pumice. The minerals flow into all sorts of other forms and then break apart again. It is a sort of rolling, moving incarnation in conjunction with the other souls, so as to gain knowledge of as many elements as possible. Although it will not experience them all it will learn enough to know how to control most physical forms.

It is certain that all take at least one experience of the mineral, even the greatest of souls. This latter point is quite interesting for in all the spheres a great soul can never pass without being noticed. In the earlier realms they are often guides to huge numbers of souls and continue to be so. They particularly help in the formation of the mineral incarnations. Their own incarnation will very rarely go unnoticed in its mineral form. It will take the being of some stone or jewel that will call to an artist. Michelangelo would go to the marble quarries and find a piece of stone that he said 'called to him'. He would know that the piece of marble had great soul and only needed his skill and artistic talent to unlock it. So great statues come into existence. Flawless gems strike deep into our hearts and the immutable quality of silver and gold fascinates us. The very best of these are always the person-ifications of great souls, old souls, those destined to be always noticed. We will meet this fact again.

There is another point in considering what choice of elements any soul takes and that is whether it is a positive or negative soul. This choice has been strengthening during the soul's journey to this point and is, by now, very noticeable. The same will happen in the mineral stages.

The positive soul tends to choose relatively quiet,

peaceful elements, things that will cause no harm, even be used to good purpose, say as good earth in which food can be grown. The negative will tend to be difficult, that is to say they choose things which are likely to be harmful, or could be harmful – fire, for instance, or noxious gases. The interesting thing is that all are needed to make any world; the positive and the negative. And so it is throughout creation. One must have the other to interact and therefore be.

You may know that your body is made up of the elements of your world. A pretty obvious fact really. It may have crossed your mind then that the particles of your body are animated by another soul. Well, yes, in a way they are, but it is no more to worry about than thousands of microbes that are at this moment using your body as a home. The souls in the mineral are using the Great Spirit's particles and you are using their housing to form your own. The soul learns control of the particles in the mineral but in more advanced incarnations it leaves this to the souls who are at that stage, and uses the completed atoms and molecules. Rather like you use bacteria to help with the workings of your digestive system. You don't worry about that, do you? Your body is one of the changes experienced by the mineral.

So if your human form is a higher state of existence it implies you have dominion over these other forms of existence. Yes, in a way you do have dominion over the atoms and molecules of the earth, but you also have RESPONSIBILITY for your dominion! A responsibility that extends to everything that you can see, animal, vegetable and mineral. When humans despoil the earth they are cutting into a soul's right to exist. That it is in a state where it is impossible for it to stand up for its own rights bears no relation to your responsibility. That it appears to be 'inanimate' does not matter one whit. Though lower on the scale of life, it still has a soul that is every bit as important as your own. True the earth is there to use, but to be used with wisdom and intelligence. I fear that what mankind is presently doing to his earth has neither quality. The chemical balance is very fine and if a false move is made it is mankind that will suffer.

This is because of the greatest of all laws of the Spiritual Universe. It has been in operation throughout all the existences we have discussed but I think shows up more plainly from now on. That law is called

CAUSE AND EFFECT.

That may seem very simple to you but it has a stronger influence over your life than any other law. It is often paraphrased on your physical world, "As ye sow, so shall ye reap". It was a symbol given in the usual way with the greatest of truths behind the giving. I call it *cause and effect* because you are more likely to be a townsperson to whom sowing and reaping will not mean much.

What it means is whatever you do, or cause to be done, there will be an effect. Not exactly an 'equal and opposite reaction' as science puts it but nevertheless, there will be an effect.

For instance, if mankind refuses to stop using some particular harmful chemical or gas it will have the inevitable effect of affecting the other chemicals or gases of your world. The law is the law in every endeavour, field of life and existence of the souls of the Great Spirit. Never doubt it. It may not appear to be so but you are not yet omnipotent and will not always witness the results of the law of cause and effect. We will undoubtedly return to the discussion of this law for it affects much more than physical particles.

And so, eventually, the smallest unit of the total soul comes to the end of its existence in physical-mineral form and has put a space between itself and its sisters. I cannot stress how important that is. This raw material is the first instance of a soul that will individualise and eventually become a human soul. Rather I should say, the soul of a human! It is what will one day become somebody like you. There are no further splitting up processes, this is what it has all been about. From now on individualisation is the most important goal of the soul. For although it is separated from its fellows it is not individual. It cannot stand, so to speak, on its own, but it is ready to learn how to do that. It is ready to progress to life, biological life in a universe that is on the physical wavelength. Of course, as we have said, that may mean many other worlds besides your own that have vegetation.

The soul now has lessons to learn in controlling new forms of completed atoms. This is done by repeated incarnations starting at the bottom of physical biological creation, the very lowest forms of vegetation such as algae, spores and lichens.

Oh dear! I hope I haven't lost you. Perhaps you have not been able to see the purpose behind these ventures into something as inanimate as mineral, let alone imagine yourself wanting to be a vegetable! I think within the next chapter or so I will make it a little plainer why these things happen and give you a reasonable explanation.

So this pre-human soul is taking its first steps in the very important business of individualisation. From now on its purpose is to grow to maturity as a single being, a single cognisance, a complete entity. This will take a very long time but not as long as the ages it has taken to get this far. This individualisation of the soul, as I have said, is the whole purpose of the gradual breakdown of the total soul we have witnessed so far. As the vegetation they are just about to become grows, flowers and seeds, these souls are the seeds of the future. They now have to prepare for their wonderful destiny. But it will be many, many incarnations of very many kinds before they even begin to have an inkling of what that destiny might possibly be. It does not matter. Its purpose at this time is just to experience and learn, and it has all the time in the world to do just that.

To give ourselves a rest from considering actual incarnations of the souls for the moment, we will talk about the construction of the various spheres we have touched upon and take this chance to look forward a little. I would now like you to consider this symbol of *The Spheres of the Spiritual Universe*. A central ring bound about by interconnecting rings. The central ring represents the Great Spirit whose presence runs throughout all creation, is all creation. The rings represent the seven spheres through which a soul will pass while making the great journey.

We can see that we have only talked about four of these spheres so far. These are represented by the top left hand ring as the Pre-Angelic realms, the second the Angelic realms, the third the etheric and the fourth is the physical where you have your residence. We have come half circle. It must occur to you that the next three rings represent spheres of living after the physical. You are quite right and I have my being in the next circle of the representation for I have done with earthly incarnations, my last being over three thousand years ago.

However, I will not spoil the story of the journey of the soul by telling you at this point exactly what lies ahead, but nor will I treat you as a fool. It is obvious that the journey will take the soul back to its starting place just as the logs returned to the centre of the fire.

Do you notice an odd thing about the three circles at the bottom of the ring? The one before the physical sphere and the one after touch each other and both are closely intertwined with the circle that represents the physical sphere. In truth all three lower rings represent one great universe. Within it reside all beings that have made this their chosen branch of the Spiritual Universe. There are numberless etheric universes and they interpenetrate all the many physical universes, all without ever disturbing one another. They are at differing places on the scale of the whole complete universe represented by the three rings.

The two rings either side of the physical ring touch

because they are made up of the same sort of particle, that is to say, etheric substances. Both are the stage outside the physical. Actually, the stage absolutely next to yours is sometimes called 'The Astral'. You may have heard of that term. It is a pre and post state that helps the soul acquire the new kind of particle, namely the physical, a sort of very dense etheric. We met with a similar stage between the energy sphere and the etheric consisting of what I termed etheric-energy particles. These stages help the soul migrate from one composition to another.

In fact the astral is so dense as to sometimes impinge on your world and hence you have the stories of ghosts, poltergeists, etc., which abound, the almost physical disturbances that can happen. It is also so dense that happenings in your world can record themselves into it and then you get the recurring apparition that walks above or below the present floor level or through walls. It never takes any notice if addressed for it is nothing but a recording. The original soul has long gone.

To return to our two etheric spheres of existence. That is exactly what they are, spheres of existence. Do not think of round spheres like your globe. It is a wavelength on the scale of creation where there are more worlds and levels of life than you could ever comprehend. All souls are found within the etheric, the pre-physical and the post-physical. You see the pre-physical are what make up the worlds we live in or on, are their mineral, Flora and Fauna. Their incarnations are what we, in the post-etheric, use and have our existence within. We use the worlds they create just as you are using the earth. We all co-exist and help each other. Why then have three rings? Because each is symbolic of the soul's different levels of existence rather than the composition of the universe in which it lives. This explanation really applies to the whole of our symbol. After all, it is only a symbol.

Chapter 4

Vegetable and Mineral

The single soul, having separated from the others of its soul-cell group, now has to learn to live alone. It takes on the life of simple vegetation, algae, lichen, mosses, spores, before moving on to more complicated vegetable life forms.

The soul finds there is now one big difference. The going in and the going out of incarnations is far harder. No gentle drifting in and out at will as the soul did in past spheres. There are certain things that have to be done to attain the incarnation, what one might almost call formulas to be gone through, before the life can be realised. At first it is quite simple but later it will become more complicated, very complicated indeed. One step at a time is taken. Now understanding the mineral elements, the soul finds out how to make the atoms do what it wants by taking the simplest of forms, often clinging to manifestations of its former likeness, or water-born single cell plants. In following lives it becomes mosses and other simple forms.

As the souls progress and learn to control these simple plants, they move up the scale to the more complex and difficult forms of life. As I have said before, these lives are not all on your world, but can range throughout the whole of your universe, some more simple than anything you have on your world and some so complex that they would confound your botanists.

In this stage, the vegetable, the soul will meet with a totally new concept, something which is of the physical universe. That is death. Never before has it had to undergo its rigours. What is different? Well before, when the time came to leave a form, the incarnator just relinquished its hold at will, *WHEN IT WANTED TO GO.* That is the biggest difference. Physical death comes when *IT* will, there is no choice in the matter. The incarnator must live in its physical form until it dies. When it dies, it must leave. This, as I have said, is a different concept, a very different way of going about things. The main reason is that the physical particles are of a very heavy nature, not so malleable by thought, once a soul is incarnate within them. This is another reason why the soul has just undergone such a long sojourn in the mineral: so that it may be accustomed to the idea of not being able to leave its form at will.

In the mineral it learned great patience, stamina that is needed in the lowest, long-lived forms of vegetation – acceptance that is needed throughout the incarnation in vegetation: it has to stay put and take whatever comes. The vagaries of the weather, lack of sustenance, the attention of the elements such as fire, and possible termination by becoming food for some higher incarnation. A sudden death.

At this kind of termination the soul is driven out, rather

than leaving when its time is accomplished and the form is no longer tenable. If it is at the normal end of the life, it will be relatively easy to accomplish, a slow withdrawal of the etheric from the physical it has been interpenetrating. Yes, it animates the plant in just the same way as you animate your own body. This is the method used by all etheric souls taking form on your physical plane of existence.

So how does the soul attach itself in the first place? That is the other great difference in physical incarnation. Before, when a soul of any stage wanted to have some life-form experience, it would attend at the world in question and observe for a while. Then it would pull to itself particles that would give it form in that world, a completed form, as often as not, an adult form. There would be no mother or father although the soul may have had what I would term sponsors, another soul or souls that would have been in close relationship to it. The conception of a progenitor and progeny is of the physical worlds, your wavelength. It starts with the vegetable form.

In most cases it has to take a seed that is formed by a parent and the soul will, so to speak, put out feelers towards the seed and begin to align itself with the atoms, interpenetrating it with its own etheric substance. It will know what shape it has to form and have a mental picture of it held in its mind. It then has to bend its own form to that of the shape it has chosen, match it, physical atom for what we will term an 'etheric atom'. There is a blue-print within the seed of the form it will be in maturity, but the incoming soul has some control of what might be termed the building operation.

Gradually it will fit into place and co-exist with the

physical. Each etheric atom will be reflected in the physical shape and vice versa. The physical needs this interpenetration of the etheric, for remember, with it comes the energy, mind and most of all, the flame of life, that particle of the Great Spirit that gives the blessing of life. Without it the seed will not develop. Yes, all these things are still residual in the soul that takes on the new form, and are completely necessary to the new plant if it is going to live.

All that the total soul, the soul-cell, has undergone was to give the soul the grounding to be able to enter and control the physical world. Now in the vegetable form, the soul learns for the first time the new entry into a life of birth and the exit of death. Even the mineral was not quite that. It is why the vegetable stage of the soul is so important. Like the mineral, one that has to be undergone before the soul can progress.

Before we move on let us look at some points about this period of existence, what it means to us. We have already discussed our responsibility to the mineral, its kinship and right to exist without being despoiled, yet we also mentioned the fact of good earth in which things can be grown. This implies that vegetable life uses the mineral to have its existence. The vegetation has the right to use the mineral elements to form its body and to be a life source. In its turn the vegetation is there as a life source to the next stage of life, the animal.

The vegetable can make no demur when the browsing animal crops the grass or leaves, it cannot complain when the monkey or the bird plucks the fruit or nut and consumes it. In fact it has learnt to make use of such things to remove its seed to a new area. Nor can it shout out loud when the human reaps the corn or pulls the turnip from the ground to make a meal. It has been shown that on a certain scale the vegetable does cry out at this treatment but it is not on the scale that upsets the eater. That the eater is clever enough to make an instrument that will tell him of this scream is not important. At the natural level it did not disturb him. It is not supposed to disturb him for it is nourishment that he must have to continue existing and is there for him as the earth is there for the vegetable.

The death of the vegetable was inevitable in time and its sudden demise is only a part of the whole. In fact by the time the grass, leaf, fruit, or whatever is eaten, the soul that gave life to the plant has gone, withdrawn back to the etheric regions. This is why the plant will immediately begin to degenerate back to its components, either inside or outside an animal. It goes back to its mineral constituents ready to be pulled into another form, possibly that of the animal that ate it. The soul of the mineral is still present but not that which inhabited the plant as a whole. It is now of a higher state of consciousness than the mineral form and although it gives up what might be termed its body as food for others, it does not have its soul incorporated in that other form. This then is another great difference in the vegetation stage of existence.

I am sure that I now do not have to spell out for thinking man why he has a duty to conserve the vegetation, the plant life of his world and make good use of it. It is one thing to use trees for necessary furniture but quite another to tear down forests for no purpose at all other than sheer greed. It is lovely for a woman to place a few flowers for her family to enjoy that have been grown for that purpose in her garden but quite another to go out and purposefully destroy rare species of wild flowers.

Food that is grown for greed and gain, then left to rot is a crime! Man has the brains to be able to solve these problems of too much for some and starvation for others. Perhaps if he can come to understand that the vegetation of his world is nothing so much as himself in an earlier form, a brother in existence, he might begin to understand what harm he is doing. I have little hope; man cannot understand that the animal is his kindred on his world or even love his own kind. Even when his own continued existence on the world is in jeopardy he will not listen. And he should pay heed to the mineral and vegetable forms of life, for within them he has his own life!

One interesting fact before we leave the world of plants. Have you ever wondered how a plant knows how to make itself look like it does? How does it know that if it constructs a pitcher, flies and insects will fall in, or what colours will attract bees and birds? How can it make its flower look like a bee? All the million and one variations it forms to survive. It does not have what might be called a brain to think. It has no eyes to observe a bee. How then can it do these things?

The answer is in what we have just discussed. It is the very fact of the incarnating soul that gives it these abilities. It is the mind that creates these myriad forms from the knowledge gained in previous lives. The basic plant is on the earth but the soul will, so to speak, redesign the plant a little. Following souls will continue to do this refining, this progression of the plant which never really ceases. This, then, is the missing link behind evolution.

Man helps the plant world when he researches to get better strains of wheat, larger fruit or even more beautiful flowers. This is a plus for mankind and a lot more has gone into it than just the earthly research. In the etheric dimensions there will have been much thought put into the progression of these vegetable forms.

* * * * *

The soul has now become much attached to incarnations in the world of the physical. It is ready to make the great leap from passive to active. By this I mean a change from a life that is generally in one place, accepting whatever presents itself, good or bad, to a life where the being is separate from his environment and can alter, have an effect on its surroundings. It can range to gather its sustenance which no longer comes directly from the mineral. In other words, zoological life. As the soul started with simple forms in the vegetable world, so it now does the same with the world of animals.

At first there is little difference in the existences except in their complexity. The soul has been used to inhabiting very sophisticated species of plant form. Its first undertaking as a zoological life-form will be as a single cell animal. Yes, a micro-organism, bacteria or virus, something invisible to the human eye.

It may seem a retrograde step but it is not. Any form of biological living tissue is a massive step forward in the soul's progression of incarnations. It has to learn a totally new way of controlling its vehicle of expression, new formulas and new mechanics. Some of these lives will be almost as static as the vegetable. Take an underwater species that attaches itself to a rock or ship for life.

You will remember that at the beginning of the vegetable incarnations the group soul-cell has broken apart but the souls contained therein stayed close by one another to make their incarnations. The same thing now happens in the animal world, but as you can imagine each soul clings just a little less closely to the others of its group than before. It is now truly a self-contained form of existence, although in a group form as in myriads of bacteria, microbes and so on. Why, I hear you ask, do we need to take these lowly forms, what is the point? To answer this I must digress a little before returning to the progress up the scale of animal life forms. In this book we are trying to show you how you came to have the gift of a human life and that it was you who gave it to yourself. What we are also trying to point out is: that this wonderful gift does not happen by a few magic words being said, the wave of a hand, or suddenly, in the twinkling of an eye. No more than anything on your world makes a sudden entrance. There is growth and development before the appearance of any life. It is by dint of long, long experience, learning, trying out and making mistakes that you come at last to have the chance to live the life of a physical animal, albeit the first tries are as single cell animals, the merest pinch of biological form. The practical reason for this is that the soul has to learn to control the most difficult of all life forms. It is heavy, cumbersome and hard to manipulate. The joining of the etheric and the physical has to be very strong, to the detriment of the etheric, in order for the soul to have 'awareness' in the solid world of the physical through the creature of its choice.

This control has to be learnt a cell at a time. A chemical, an element at a time. First one then two, then more. From every incarnation since the mineral, the soul has had more and more complicated forms to control. Gradually, painfully slowly, it learns the mechanics of the physical and how it works. It sets this knowledge in its memory so that the next and the next time it can use it without giving too much thought to it. Its digestive system, for instance, cell making, circulation, breathing, metabolism and so much more. Hormones, secretions, chemical messengers. The nervous system and the brain. All, all have to be learnt, as you say, by heart. Do you ever think about your digestion other than when it is painful? Your breathing? Or take the chemical balance of your body and a million or more things that go on inside you everyday without ever a conscious thought of your own.

Ah, you say, that comes under the control of the subconscious mind. Where do you think the control of that 'subconscious' mind comes from? Where did the knowledge that is in that subconscious come from? Even if it was all there, ready for you to use when you were born, from whence came the ability to be able to use it? I'll tell you and I don't care how unprovable it is. It comes from the thousands of times you have entered and left life-forms of a different kind both before your physical universe and also on your plane of existence. Without them you could not be the 'You' you are today!

You are a wonder, a delight, most precious, for you have proved your tenacity and ability. You have wrung the right to your human life through undergoing the whole gamut of experience and garnered ability in the numberless times you have subjected yourself to the experience of life. You are the beloved of this universe and the Spiritual Universe for what you have done. Does this go some way to answering the 'Why' of all those mineral and vegetable incarnations?

This then is meant to be a practical book although we undoubtedly will be looking at the ethics and moral questions of life in later chapters, so please remember that having a practical outlook, gaining knowledge of how you work, is not disrespectful to the Great Spirit. Only It knows the effort of will each one of us puts into the purpose of our existence and we are supported and loved for that effort. Even when we don't know we have made these gargantuan endeavours, we are still making them every second we exist. Now I am going to continue to tell you how you did it and to what purpose.

And so we started at the bottom of the animal world to learn the business of control of the body until it became second nature to us. First learning to be cells that divide to increase in number. Here one soul teaches another how to form itself and read the blue-print. Then up through the world of simple creatures, mostly underwater, some would have been microbe beings on dry land. Again I remind you not to limit your ideas of existence to your world alone but let your imagination roam freely to encompass a vast range of worlds on which the soul might choose to have an incarnation.

After experiencing the forms of animal life that do not increase their numbers by some form of fertilised seed, the soul moves on to learn exactly this kind of life-form. It learns to attach itself at the moment of conception, however that is performed by each species. The soul takes over the two cells made by the parents who relinquish them to its use, a gift to the future generation. It then goes on to use the blue-print within those cells to build its new body, its vehicle of expression in the physical world. It has learnt the rudiments of this in the vegetable form and now it does the same thing in the animal kingdom.

You must be thinking, is this the same for us humans, after all we are animals? The answer is yes. In fact all life forms on your world use similar methods of expressing themselves on your plane of the physical. Once contact is made with the seed the soul builds the body by the same interpenetrating method I have described, the soul using to create form in the vegetable existence. There is no other way a soul can incarnate on a physical world by its very nature. This is the method, the modus operandi of physical incarnations.

Slowly the kinds of bodies chosen would become more complex. They would become all kinds of animals from crustacea to insects, from fish to reptile, from bird to mammal. I do not mean necessarily in that order, or that any one soul becomes every one of them, but it will have some experience of every group. Which it chooses depends very much on the soul in question.

By this time the nature of the soul is more evident in its choice of incarnation according to whether its polarity is positive or negative. I do not mean by this whether its choice is female or male for it will be male in some lives and female at other times. The positive and negative we are talking about does not manifest in this way. Rather I am talking about the benevolent and the malicious. Those taking the positive path will generally appear in the form of some benign animal life form. Something calm, non-belligerent and not dangerous. Do not think the positive soul will not have lives where it is carnivorous and will kill to eat. That is something we all have to experience both as the eater and the eaten. If you shudder at the pictures on your TV of nature in the raw, an insect biting off the head of another, the lion killing, then that repugnance shows the progress you have made. The negative souls will tend to choose such lives and revel in the carnality of them.

Killing, depriving others of their body, does seem to be the lowest thing to which any life form can stoop. Yet it is a part of nature on your plane of existence. One form gives

up its body as food for another. It starts in the mineral
where as an atom it will become part of some other life
form, sometimes two or three, one after the other as each
is ingested by the other. As we said, in that form the soul
does not vacate the incarnation because this happens.
Later in the vegetable form it often gives up its body for
sustenance and learns for the first time about sudden
death. It also learns sacrifice, a most important lesson.

In the animal form it is driven by the law of survival to
kill or be killed. To fight to defend or gain. In fact it is the
very powerful nature of instinct that is used to teach the
soul many lessons. It is here that we should learn to
overcome the desire to kill, but somehow we do not.

Not only is the positive-negative side of the soul's
nature a factor in its choice of body and life, but also
whether the soul is a brash new soul or one of the ancients
passing through this branch of creation.

The new soul will not only have lives that are
surrounded by its soul-mates but it will stay in the
primitive forms much, much longer. As it progresses it
will always tend to be in forms such as bees, wasps, shoals
of fish, herds of animals. This is the reason why such
animals have what is referred to as 'herd instincts'. They
are joined together by more than instinct. They still have a
direct relationship to each other in which there is an
enforced separation during the incarnation into separate
bodies and, after death, a return to the etheric dimensions
and companionship of their group soul to rest.

Each time the soul incarnates it gains a little more
experience of looking after itself and being independent.
The height of independence for this young type of soul is
as grazing animals in their most complicated form.

Can you see all the things the soul has to learn during

its sojourn in the animal world? From how to manipulate the physical forms, to learning its first lessons in individuality and responsibility for its own life.

It is not quite so necessary for older souls to be in groups as it is for young souls, although they will choose some lives in these forms. Often it will be as the leaders of such groups. They will have a particular fondness for some souls whom they have been guiding while on their own journey. This guiding is the responsibility of these older souls. Almost every soul that is not a completely new total soul when it leaves the Great Spirit is the guide for some other soul and even the new soul will be a helpmate and friend to its neighbours. We do not pass through all the spheres of the Spiritual Universe on our own. We make friends, have relationships of all kinds. Relationships that last for aeons of time. Friendships that you will even now still be experiencing in your own life, and that were made when you left the heart of the universe. You will, in all likelihood, be a guide to some other soul.

The older souls, the ones whom I mentioned as not breaking down any further than into soul-cells, they will always appear in what might be called a more forceful incarnation. Either as animals that lead lone lives like pandas, bears, snakes, or in group animals they will be the queen bees, the elephant matriarch, the dominant member of any group. They will give leadership wherever they incarnate. Yet be sure that they too have things to learn and come to earth for the same reasons as the younger soul. No form of life will be missed by them but they may not stay in each stage so long. Progression will be quicker through the various necessary incarnations.

There is one other way you as a human can recognise

these great ones. Have you ever noticed that occasionally some wild animal will consort with man? A dolphin will come to a beach and play with the bathers. A tiger will come out of the forest and not hurt man. A wild bird decides to come to humans for its sustenance. When this happens, be sure this is the incarnation of a great soul. The more spectacular the interaction with humans the greater is the soul. It could even be one of the rarest, a single soul making its pilgrimage through the animal kingdom. Believe me, the soul animating that animal may be so far in advance of your own that you would not even be able to stay in its company if it were out of the physical incarnation. It does not mean that because a soul is in a lower form of incarnation to you that it is necessarily below you in knowledge and progression. This is one of the great facts, the great lessons we must learn. Respect and tolerance begins here. The right of every soul to its particular incarnation and humility to know when to bow to the fuller expression of the Great Spirit. For that is what these great souls are. As I have said before, they never pass without being noticed in any form that they take.

After many sojourns in the animal kingdom the soul has learnt its lessons and comes to a point where it has total control over its body and a little capacity to spare. It is ready to take some of the last of its forms in this period of animal incarnation. The spare capacity is part mental power, part love.

During this period the soul has been learning something quite new. Care for another being to the detriment of itself. Of course this has been done again, by instinct; another lesson that is forced upon the soul. That strongest of all instincts, reproduction and survival of the species. Mostly as a female, it has learnt to love and care for its baby. Sometimes as a male it has had to learn to care for its mate or group. Fight for them, die for them. Would you believe that this caring, this first taste of responsi-bility, this first expression of love is what the journey of the soul has been all about?

No, I don't expect you do. It almost seems too small a thing to even notice. Yet it is the biggest, most important thing on our journey through the Spiritual Universe. That and the individualisation of the soul.

Oddly, although the total soul was comprised of love at the start of its journey, the broken down parts of soul-cells and souls lose sight of this as they cloak down into coarser and coarser particles. It is, as I have said many times, at the centre of their being. Yet the knowledge of love and its expression is what they have come to find. Of course, as in all things, there are many other forms of knowledge that have to be sought and acquired, will be needed, but most of them are in order that 'love' may be garnered, brought home. In the animal form we see the dawn of that marvellous moment when the soul finds that for which it has come so far to seek. But it still has so far to go. It has to learn how to bring that love through all the layers of its being and express it, then find out how to take that store of love with it on the return journey.

During its last incarnations as an animal it often gives the responsibility for its development to you. You as a human being. Yes, these are the animals that consort with you from simple cattle to clever dogs. Can you guess one of the things you do to help develop these animals? It is that you give them a name. Even if it is only Pig 129, Crumple Horn or Bonzo. Whatever it is, you mean that animal and no other. This has never happened before. Humans often write tales about animals and give them names, making the animals call each other by the name. This anthropormorphising does not happen. Only humans call an animal by a name. The name you give an animal is the first it has ever had and it confers true individuality, the very thing the soul has been struggling to achieve.

Do you have a dog? Lucky you. Study yours now or any other pet that you may own. Perhaps it seems to think it owns you and has become very attached to you. It shows an emotion akin to love. Stories abound of dogs that die of broken hearts when their master or mistress dies. This is absolutely true and it means that its keeper did his or her duty to that animal. For they brought out in that soul a feeling, a non physical, mental feeling, emotion that so pervaded it that it even gave up its incarnation to follow its owner. Something against all instinct to survive.

This or something like it is the true moment of the soul turning towards the long journey home to the Great Spirit. It is exactly on the opposite side of the circle of life. In its heaviest moment of incarnation in matter it has found its own heart. Now it has to learn to express that heart.

Can you see how important is the animal existence? Your overwhelming responsibility not only for its continuance and well-being, but your duty to any animal in your care is to bring out those feelings of love by showing love yourself. Think carefully about it, for the next estate of the soul is as homo sapiens, mankind. Without the animals – no man would ever appear. Somewhere, sometimes you and I, learnt that lesson and won the right to become a homo sapiens. Probably we were helped by another soul to turn homewards, progress to the next stage of life form, where although still an animal, we would have mental powers that would allow us to begin to learn how to express what is at the heart of every one of us.

Chapter 5

And so to Humanity

The Dawn of Time. What does that conjure up for you? The world still a moving, heaving mass of volcanoes and earthquakes. Prehistory, primeval forests and plains. A little later only animals of strange and wondrous size, reptiles and odd birds with no feathers. Not a trace of mankind anywhere. That is an accurate picture of the dawn of time on your planet. Your scientists make finds every day to confirm this. They are also making finds that say man has been on earth longer than was previously thought, living in cohesive families, civilised structure. But before that, what was man then? He was an animal, like any other, going about his business, developing himself on your planet. What was it that made this animal, 'like any other', different?

Size of brain, you might immediately answer. And correctly. Its upright stance. True. Its digital ability. True again. But even before that was apparent, was there anything to recommend this animal, that it should have dominion over all the world?

I am afraid it is one of those 'Yes and No' answers. You see, it was known from previous experience that this kind of animal had the potential to develop all these gifts and because of this it was chosen. Yes, chosen. By whom? By the souls who wanted to inhabit such bodies, souls in the etheric regions who had of necessity to live a particular sort of life in order to be able to make progress on their journey.

All this may seem far fetched and confusing so let's take it a step at a time. Your wheel of the Spiritual Universe was not always in existence nor will it always be in existence. The Pre-Angelic realms, the Angelic realms are always there but, as you will remember, when the soul gets to the etheric regions it chooses which universe it will journey through. We have chosen the Etheric/Physical Universe, you and I.

The first soul-cells to choose this branch would have found a totally new universe and they would have begun to make it what it is. The passage of time would have brought uncountable numbers of soul-cells and souls to pass through the universe and each one would leave its mark, move it forward just a little more, push the boundaries out a little further. Some of these souls would have been very experienced from previous journeys through other universes and would use that experience to shape the new etheric and physical universes that they found. They would do this by incarnations in those universes. This shaping is still happening today, at this very moment, in your universe.

Now you might think that this implied that the shaping was what might be termed 'Good', to the benefit of all. This is manifestly not true, you have only to look about your world to see this, read its history. There is an awful lot of what could be equally termed 'Bad'. This is because the physical branch appears to attract more than its fair share of the negative souls. Why this is, is not fully known except that your physical sphere offers the negative full scope for its needs and desires. Now this may seem a desperately terrible thing that a whole universe should suffer from this over-weight of negative souls but it equally means that enormous lessons can be wrung from a preponderance of what is often thought of as 'Evil'.

Now hold in your mind, as we look at how your actual planet became the home of mankind, that even in your own universe there are other forms of life. Outside your universe there are myriads more, many of a more positive nature and some as negative as your own. Regretfully I must tell you there are fewer of the latter. This does not mean your universe is loved any the less by the Great Spirit or that it does not produce that which is needed by the Great Spirit. All is one within It and as I have said before, it appears that both positive and negative are needed for the Spiritual Universe to continue to exist. It does mean that we have to work a lot harder to obtain that for which we came and anything that is hard to win is always worth that much more than something easily obtained. Keep that in mind as well, for it might seem at times that I offer a counsel of despair. Also remember, you, in your total soul stage, helped make the choice of which universe you and your soul-mates would journey through and there would have been a good reason for the choice.

But to return to the planet earth, that tiny portion of not only the Spiritual Universe but of your own universe. When the first soul-cells ventured into the new universe they had found ready to be developed, they would have become the equivalent of your minerals, vegetables and so on, in the etheric parts of that universe. There would have to be souls taking on these forms to bring the universe into existence. Where the original material comes from is not really known except to the Great Spirit. Some think it is provided by It in what might be called raw form. Others say it consists of particles of other universes that have broken down and are ready to be reused. Whichever it is, total souls on their journey would find the right conditions to create a new wheel of life. Gradually it is formed and extended as souls plunge deeper into possibilities, exploring how the new universe can be used to generate continuity of the whole. Etheric worlds are formed of heavier and heavier material, particles. Lives would be lived on these worlds and each time a soul came out of an incarnation it would find itself attracted to the next heavier density of particle.

It is the same law that we discussed before in a previous realm, being used to drive the soul onward. Each incarnation leaves the soul with a heavier form of particle within its make-up and the soul cannot return to lighter forms, only the same again or denser. Eventually these souls would encounter the deepest form of incarnation in your universe, namely yours, the physical. But it would not have been as beings such as yourselves, for at first such beings would not have existed.

These first souls in your branch of the Spiritual Universe would have been trail blazers. Most would be old and experienced souls who would come into the universe, carry out the task they had come to do and then most would return to the Great Spirit from whatever level they had got to, as there would be no possibility of an earth-type life yet. And some of these older souls would stay as long as the universe existed. Those returning would have been able to gather what it was they came for, laboured mightily for it, just as you are doing now. These souls would have touched very near the physical level, deep into the etheric regions. They were the architects of your universe.

There are others that are still with you in mineral form. They would have been souls wishing to take that step in existence. They have been with you since the dawn of your earth time and will be there till its end.

Once the mineral was formed, some souls would venture to be the first life on earth, such as vegetable, and later animal. They would do this as the conditions appeared that allowed this to happen. Very slowly each soul brought its experience to bear and developed the different species. As new ones were formed they would be tested to see if they had that certain something for which these souls were searching, that certain something that would yield a return. It is known that somewhere every universe has a form that will yield the fuel, that is necessary for the soul to find, in smaller or larger quantities. On your world it turned out to be the animal now known as homo sapiens. Don't think you were the first species to be tried out for you were not. But you were the species that, shall we say, worked out.

Now the older souls, as I have said, sometimes gathered fuel from the universe as they found it. Because of their great knowledge and experience they could do this. But hoards of lesser souls would have followed them into the new universe for there are always those looking for ways to express themselves. They would be dragged down the descending ladder of denser incarnations but they would not know how to extricate themselves. This would have been aeons after the birth of your branch of the universe. It would be quite well developed by this time. These souls would have passed their mineral existence elsewhere and have come to pass through the vegetable and animal phase of existence. When they had gone through all that was offered by the physical, they found that they still had not found that certain something. Greater souls were consulted, for as I have said, there is always guidance for those who ask.

It was explained that it needed a certain kind of animal which had greater abilities in which they must incarnate to gain the knowledge they needed. To me this shows the infinite wisdom of the Great Spirit. It does not provide a finished article, a universe, a world, a being, for the souls to use. It makes them form these things out of the particles It provides. These particles work according to Its laws and within those laws the souls work out their destinies. The Great Spirit did not 'make man'. Mankind made man. But, remember, the soul is the Great Spirit. A paradox I know but just another way of looking at things.

So here are pre-mankind souls, obviously not yet called mankind, looking at your world from theirs, the etheric, looking for this elusive form that might exist and could be used to a new and greater purpose than just an animal incarnation. As I have said, others were tried but not found to be suitable. Somewhere, some time, the forbears of homo sapiens were found and tried out.

How many times do you wonder on your earth world why it was that man was so successful where others failed? Why did he stand up on two legs, which did not benefit him physically, for it is the source of constant ill health in your species? Why did he develop the use of tools? Why is his brain bigger? So many question marks stand over his entry into the history of your planet and the late stage that he appeared, and over the phenomenal speed of his progress in ability and knowledge, leaving all other species behind in the mists of time. Oh yes, they have refined, progressed a little, but nothing like homo sapiens, mankind.

The reason lies outside the boundaries of your world; before the dawn of your time. The answer lies deep in your very soul. For it was the soul, maybe not exactly your soul but ones much like it, that caused that change in your species. Having found an animal that looked promising there would have been experiments led by experienced souls in incarnating into that pre-human species. This would have been remarkably uncomfortable for the advanced souls but it would not have been any more uncomfortable or difficult for the younger souls than for any other animal. Indeed less progressed souls were, of course, already inhabiting these animals or they would not have existed, but they would have been of a lower order, still deep in their animal series of incarnations which they would have continued elsewhere.

Do you recall how I mentioned in the world of vegetation, the soul would redesign the plant just a little, possibly improving its chances of survival. Well, the same principle goes on in the animal world, and it can be enhanced and brought forward if great concentration is given to it by the souls in the etheric, particularly if those souls are of great knowledge. This then is what happened to the pre-human animal.

Can you imagine what it must have been like for some great soul of enormous knowledge and developed consciousness to have to live a life as one of these primitive animals? It hardly bears thinking about, yet that is precisely what happened. These superior etheric beings

incarnating in these bodies gave that evoltic push that
made homo sapiens. They redesigned the body over
thousands and thousands of the short life spans of the
animal until it developed into the sentient being with
brain capacity to spare. Capacity and the time to ponder,
'Why am I here?' – 'What is it all about?' – 'Who am I?'.

When this happened the great souls would have done
their work, and incarnating in the bodies of mankind
would be the souls of those who had sought this kind of
life. The questions they asked were the progress that they
sought, although they did not know that was what they
had been seeking. All the questions they asked were
important but the last question most of all, for in the fact
that they asked that question resided the achievement of
all that had gone before. It meant that they had arrived at
the point of:

INDIVIDUALISATION.

They had discovered within themselves that which I
told you about at the start of our discussions: the 'I exist'
principle within all of us that is our very soul, the particle
of the Great Spirit. That spark which never goes out
however deeply we descend into the densest of matter
and lose complete sight of our source. It was, is and will
always be there. In the body of a being called a homo
sapiens, the soul can rediscover this fact, be dimly aware
of its purpose, its pilgrimage, and reach out towards its
future, its heritage, its right, and at last, start making the
return journey home.

It may seem strange that we come from light and love
only to lose sight of it. The total soul that is perfection in
everything, except that it is separated from its source, has
to undergo this breakdown into constituent parts. Yet if it
did not do this, it would not be able to pick up the

nutriments, the fuel for which it came. Only in this broken down form with all its parts individually recognising themselves can the complete soul begin to gather that which is vital to continuity of the whole of the Spiritual Universe. It enables it to combine, or recombine with basic particles of energy-knowledge-love, and in this recombined form have the ability to take it forward. We will consider this more fully in another chapter, for now I want you to realise that we have reached not only the most important part of our soul's history but the part of the book for which you have been waiting, about earth life and thereafter.

* * * * *

How long does a soul have to keep coming back to have a physical life or one similar elsewhere? If we are speaking of reincarnation, is it as some schools of Eastern thought postulate, that it is very regular and you are back within forty days of your last death, or is it longer? What about the teaching of progression until you have reached 'Nirvana' and do not return to earth again?

The answer is one of our 'tis and 'tisn'ts. You see, everything depends on the soul in question. Is it an old soul, one of the great ones? Or is it a young soul with little experience? Is it of the positive or negative path? Has it learnt what it was supposed to learn and when tried out on earth, did it appear to have remembered what it had learnt? All these things must be taken into consideration. Some will only have a very few lives and pass on up the wheel of life quite quickly. Others will be caught up in the slough of physical living and spend hundreds of lifetimes on your earth or others. Remember, years ago life was often much much shorter than the seventy years now thought to be less than normal. I myself died at approximately the age of twenty-eight and I had no earthly cares, I had everything that a man could desire. Everything but a body that I could continue to hold together. I who made laws was subject to a greater law the law of easy corruptibility of the physical.

Modern man lives far longer than I did and future man will live even longer. That is if man manages to learn to use his earth correctly. This is the great doubt, the great question. Yet even if he does not and brings about the destruction of his own race by his own hand, it will only be the race of homo sapiens that he will have destroyed. It will only be his world, his planet, the planet earth, that he will have destroyed. He will not have destroyed the physical universe. That will still be there. And all it will mean is that the souls who inhabit this universe of the physical sphere and its etheric spheres will have to find somewhere else to have their existences. Even if the whole physical wheel of creation was no more, it would only mean that the souls using it would have to go elsewhere.

This may seem a theory of disposable universes. This is not so. Every wheel of the creation is there for a purpose, and if it was no more, then a similar one producing its particular type of fuel would have to be created. Its type of fuel is obviously needed by the Great Spirit. Remembering the law of 'Cause and Effect', it would mean that those who so misused their home would have to pay for what they had done, make restitution for the damage. For 'Whatsoever a man soweth, that shall he also reap'. For those who devastated a whole branch of life, a whole world, restitution would be on a cosmic scale.

Further down the line, individually, we still are subject to this law as much as the law of physical corruptibility. This then has its effect on how many lives we lead, what estate they are and what we make of them. For although they are a time of seeing if we have learnt what we should, they are, at the same time, a school. What some term 'The School of Life'. An excellent phrase, for it is said, and I think it is true, that what is learnt while in the physical is worth many times more than what is learnt in the etheric and before. That is because the knowledge learnt in the physical is so hard won. It is learnt mainly through suffering and pain, something endemic of the earth and all physical incarnations, because of the easy corruptibility of the animal body.

And how long it seems to you that you are held in this corruptible body. Seventy years appears to be eternity. Well, it isn't! It is an eyeblink in eternity. A pinch of life. A mere nothing in the cosmic scheme. There is a little symbolic picture that goes something like this -

There is a bird that comes every thousand years to a mountain made of rock and it sharpens its beak on the rock. When the rock is completely worn away, a moment of eternity will have passed.

It is a good picture of an idea impossible to describe in words. And your life is equal to about just one of those sharpenings of the bird's beak. This may make it seem insignificant, and taken in the context of your whole existence since you left the Great Spirit I suppose it is. Yet you cannot go forward without it, or one exactly like it. If you do not succeed in doing whatever it was you set out to do when you undertook your life, you will have to find another similar one, and another, until you do do whatever it is that you must do. For it is certain that at your stage of development there would have been a purpose and a reason to your coming into your body. You had been working towards it in the etheric for great lengths of time, far longer than you would live the earthly life, for your etheric and physical lives are very closely interwoven, they are one of another, not separate.

Do you remember we posed the question 'Did the physical or the etheric come first?' and I said the etheric, but other things came before that. Now you have the answer in full.

Before the physical came the etheric via the etheric-energy. Before that the energy, and prior to that the energy-mind leading back to the mind, coming in turn from that pure radiant source of everything, The Great Spirit. So much to make one blade of grass, one ear of corn, one tree, one snake, one dog. And you as you, a human. How can you ever think you are not important? That your life is insignificant or is not WORTH living!

So the number of times you live, reincarnate as a human, differs with every individual. Whatever number is required to attain – obtain that which is needed – is the answer.

Finally, as in all the forms of life that are undertaken, there comes a moment when the soul is ready to move back entirely into the etheric regions, the etheric sphere. The soul will have the final death. It will leave the physical sphere, probably never to return. I say probably because there are always the paradoxes in creation. If I say 'Never to return' there is always likely to be the exception. But usually, it is forever on this particular journey.

This does not mean that the soul is now in a very high state of ecstasy, has reached Nirvana. Anything but. Some will be on a higher level of spiritual progress it is true, and the soul will undoubtedly be of a spiritual nature for that is the sign that it is ready to leave off having earth lives. And by spiritual, I do not mean religious in your worldly sense. It has its practical side, as ever, and its mental-spiritual sides, a combination that means the soul has found that for which it sought, that for which it came, and now it has to learn how to transport it home.

Chapter 6

First Human Incarnations

Now we are on the upward swing of the journey. We have passed the lowest and the furthest point away from where we started on the wheel of the Great Spirit. The physical universe is the most important moment in a soul's journey for it is when it first incarnates in the body of homo sapiens. It may be male or female, it matters naught, for both are equal in the pilgrimage of the soul.

The soul has been one or the other sex during its physical existences and now it will carry on being either in the next series of incarnations. Once we start talking about humans we come across the literary problem of calling a human 'he' or 'she'. You will probably have noticed that I have called the total souls, soul-cells and souls 'It' so we did not run into this problem. But it is cumbersome to put he or she every time I mention humans and tedious to read. The trouble is that when you choose one, the other feels you have left them out or have slighted them in some way. So, for the sake of convenience when I am talking about

humans, and because it is the convention, I will write 'he'.
It is nearly always expressed that way – but never, never
doubt that 'he' equally means 'she'. Please remember -
*THERE IS NO DIFFERENCE IN THE SOUL
INCARNATING IN A MALE OR FEMALE BODY!*
Neither is superior, neither is inferior.

The men must get over their long-standing feelings of
dominance and the women must cease to feel their status
is being threatened by such convention. Either that or I
shall have to call you all 'It' and both sexes can be cross
with me.

From now on we are really face to face with the premise
of reincarnation of what you call the 'human soul'. Now
you may be able to see how well this premise fits in with
all that we have discussed. I have talked about nothing
else but reincarnation right from the word go. From the
moment the total soul left the Great Spirit, it has stepped
in and out of one life after another. If this is so, do you
think this pattern would suddenly be suspended in your
physical world? If you had needed all those hundreds, no
thousands of lives to get this far, do you think you could
learn all there is to know about the most important part of
your journey in just one lifetime?

It is not possible, and the law of multi-lives to gain
experience applies to humans on your world as much as
any others in the Spiritual Universe. I must ask you to
bear with me if you find this difficult to accept for I cannot
make the truth any different because you think it should
be. I hope by this point in our dialogue, the idea that you
have passed time in other earthly-type lives is beginning
to seem reasonable. If not, follow me a little further and I
may drop some pearl that will convince you.

Let us return to that moment when homo sapiens

began to leave the other animals behind to take on a new role as a very special vehicle in which the soul could experience the lessons it needed to learn. We had left the soul at that moment in animal life where it had felt love for another creature and a tiny spark of realisation that it existed as an entity.

After each incarnation as an animal, of whatever species, it would have returned to the etheric dimensions to rest and recuperate. It would have joined its group to discuss all that had happened to it and take advice as to what to do next. This can be done in the etheric by thought transference. Words are not needed.

Usually the group would all be at about the same level of attainment, although some would be dragging behind, while others forged ahead. Previously when the souls returned to the etheric they would join very closely together. But there would never be a complete gathering of all the souls, for some would be away, incarnating. Gradually during the animal lives, each time the soul returned it would be less coalescent with its fellow souls, more individual, and later, it would be unable to rejoin them as it had before but would just be in the same vicinity, enjoying the others' company, consulting and learning from their experiences. If it were not for this group each individual would have to have every conceivable incarnation itself. But through the group it can imbibe the experiences of the others and cut down its number of lives to obtain that which it must have.

There would come a moment when the individual soul reached that point where its next life needs to be at the level of a human being. It will always have guidance at this time from a greater soul, for it is a very important moment.

Maybe you are imagining that this life will be as a human type such as yourself, developed, civilised, intelligent and educated. It is not. The first incarnation will be as a primitive type of human. This might give you the picture of a tribesman in Africa, Australia, South America, New Guinea. It will not be the right picture. When I say primitive I mean something little more than an animal. The tribal primitive is a well developed representative of mankind with customs, laws and family cohesion. He is a million years beyond the manlike animal I am talking about.

Now it must be manifestly obvious that there are no longer any such animals on your earth in which a soul could incarnate. Right. Then if all this is a continuous stream of souls passing through the universe, where do those at this point incarnate? That is why I say 'human type'.

Long ago, when the souls brought the pre-human animal into pre-eminence, as it came out of the animal stage it would have been the primitive human of which I speak. Souls would have then incarnated in these early humans and gained that very primitive experience. Later when this type of primitive was no longer on your earth, souls who came along after they had gone would have had to look elsewhere for a life form at a similar stage of development. As we have said, there are others within the universe.

The souls that lived in the primitive human body might have waited until homo sapiens also developed and then returned for another life, or equally gone off to find a more developed species elsewhere. If homo sapiens had not developed as hoped, then the souls would have gone anyway to another world where they would have sought the vehicle they needed. But mankind did develop and the souls of that period would have gone on using them, progressing with every incarnation. Remember there is always a possible interchange of incarnations with other worlds on the same or near same wavelength. Do not limit yourself to thinking 'my world' is the only one.

As it happened, the animal, homo sapiens, once started on his superior development, took giant leaps forward. In a very short time there were no more truly primitive forms of the animal and the period of their use for this moment in a soul's journey was over. It may have been that you were one of those souls who used the primitive animal form of mankind for your early man-type incarnations and have followed its progression, incarnating every so often as progression occurred until you reached the point you needed. Some of you alive today are those souls. But some, as I have just said, who have arrived at this point on their journey since primitive man disappeared from the earth, have had that particular type of life elsewhere. When these souls come to you to incarnate on your earth, after their primitive lives elsewhere, then they will most likely be the tribesmen of your world.

You can surely see that even these tribesmen are fast disappearing, being assimilated into modern mankind. Yes, even their time is at an end. The souls will have to look elsewhere, to another world with its different form of evolution and experience that before coming to your earth. This very fact will be returned to later as it is having an effect on your world as you know it, an effect that once known might help you to understand what is happening and why.

After a period as a primitive, you can see that the soul moves on up the ladder of mankind. By the time it reaches the status of tribesman it is very developed. True homo sapiens. This is because the soul is living in a society, yet individual. By this time totally individual. Each time it leaves its human body it returns, as before, to the etheric planes of existence. At first it will meet and recognise its soul-mates but as time goes on the recognition will only be that it knew them from the life it has just led. They were its family, friends, tribe, nation, and it will have a feeling towards them. A feeling it will translate as love, affection, caring about them.

Here I must say a word about the soul-cell or group to which the soul belongs. Although the soul has individualised it continues to have his life both incarnate in the physical and in the etheric near the others of its group. They are a constant source of love, help and upliftment to each other. Although with individualisation the soul loses track of the fact that they are the same group, he never loses touch with them. Some wander and stray, but the thread that joins them, rather like the silver cord that joins the physical and etheric during physical life, never breaks. Yes joined, though it might be better described as a network of energy rather than a thread.

This energy field is the residual body of the soul-cell from which the souls developed and the still higher mind body of the total soul. That mind of the total soul is still of the Great Spirit and conscious of It, though broken down into its constituent parts. Can you see, it is by this network of your higher, pre-selves that you have a connection directly to the Great Spirit? It is through this network that that which you call prayer reaches the great central heart. Also know that today, right now in your body, with knowledge, you can receive help and wisdom from this total self of a most wonderful nature.

In earlier lives as animals that network was the herd consciousness, the hive consciousness. It was what pulled the soul back to its place in the etheric. In the early primitive human form it works in the same manner but, as the soul individualises, it changes. Tribesmen recognise it less than the primitive and once the soul leaves that type of life behind the knowledge of its existence is forgotten. All that is left is a strong attraction, a feeling when two individual souls meet who belong to the same group, in the physical and in the etheric.

In the primitive, the soul moves forward in knowledge. In the tribesman he begins to learn something really new. As a modern man, and by that I mean all peoples who have had a civilisation that is more than a mere tribe going back three to four thousand years or more, he must begin to reach for the higher understanding of the spirit or soul self.

You see, up until now one civilisation was much like another. It taught the soul the lessons of that kind of existence where individuals co-operate together. There is a change that is happening, is about to happen, at this time in your history. It is the next step in the development of homo sapiens and very important. This century of yours, the twentieth, has encompassed the preparations although there were a few during the nineteenth century. Does that seem a long time? It is nothing in eternity. It has taken millions of earth years and lives to get you to this point. A mere one or two hundred years is a very short time.

The important thing to note in the above paragraph is mankind learning to 'co-operate together'. Up until now in the physical incarnations each soul was very busy learning to be individual. Sometimes that means selfish –

quite often actually! Now in the etheric, the soul is used to co-operating, and it is odd that it is pushed into the non-co-operation of animal life. It arrives into the bodies of mankind in what might be called a total shutdown. A shutdown of co-operation, a shutdown of memory. Why this is so is misunderstood and is rather difficult to get through to you.

Let's try a symbol. When a child is learning its lesson there comes a time to close the book which holds all the information and to see if the lessons have been learnt by heart. Often this sets the lesson in its mind forever, more surely than continued study.

Human type life is just that. You are seeing if you remember all you have learnt and then, you have the work, the task, of breaking out of that blindness and climbing out of that long dark valley of the physical. The man or woman that you are at this moment is homo sapiens of the highest order so far. You have had as many incarnations as was needed to bring you to this point and if necessary, you will have some more. If the evolved type of homo sapiens is no longer available on your particular world, then it will be elsewhere that your requirement will be satisfied. But it will still be within your physical sphere. The same wavelength on which you are presently operating.

When you come to the end of your present life you will 'die' in precisely the way I described in the first chapter and pass to the etheric dimensions. Here you will find all that I described, and your loved ones.

The difference between the completely individualised soul and the pre-individualised soul is that the latter stay together and cling to one another, both in the etheric and the physical. The love between them is as natural as loving ourselves. Indeed in a sense they are loving themselves. Anything the soul does for another of his soul-mates would have been of direct benefit to itself or its group.

In complete individualisation the soul is asked to do something for someone else which might have no benefit whatsoever to itself. And that someone may not even be of their own group. This seems to generate the basis of the fuel that the soul must find and learn to carry, like the returning bee to the hive. But that fuel is intangible, insubstantial and invisible. It is hard to quantify and impossible to describe in actuality. It is seen to manifest its presence in many ways but it cannot be measured or held, at least not in any of the realms that I have so far seen or visited.

All life-forms change and develop and then sometimes they die away again. This is why the soul will travel the whole universe looking for a chance to have the incarnation that will suit it at that precise moment in its own development. That development is both practical and, what your world terms, spiritual. I mean the development of the personality, the emotions and ethics. You, as a person now incarnated on earth, developed your practical ability to form and hold together a physical body a very long time ago.

Just consider all that goes into keeping your body working without a thought consciously directed at it. Every day you gasp at the wonders of chemistry that are constantly working in your system. Your scientists are now understanding more and more, your doctors working miracles of healing because of this new knowledge. You play around with the very gene of life itself, that which you call DNA. It is all very wonderful

Soul Trek

and all the more so when I tell you that the animal body is the hardest form to keep together, live within, express yourself through, than any you have ever used yet throughout the whole universe and the Spiritual Universe. It is because it is so corruptible! It falls apart at the slightest thing. How it lasts its three score years and ten, and now even longer, is very nearly a miracle. But nothing is that in all the wheel of creation. Everything that is, is always within the laws of the Great Spirit. They are never suspended for any reason, or any person, or any soul.

Here you are, existing on earth, living, loving, working, surviving, growing and learning, particularly the last thing. It is something that should be inscribed on your heart, 'Learning is one of the purposes of life'. Even you, living in a human body, and not having to think how it works, spend time making it work. For this, too, is necessary learning for future existences. Yes indeed, I am now using that knowledge gained to live the life I now pursue.

Chapter 7

Entering and Leaving the Physical

If you have been following me thus far it must be clear that there is a sequence to all that I have told you, a thread of common happenings in each dimension of your past. That common thread is a continuity of each happening leading to the next. *NOTHING EVER GOES BACKWARDS – RETURNS TO A FORMER STATE.* It has never done so from the moment the total soul left the Great Spirit until this juncture, so why should it start doing so now? We have discovered a wonderful law of continuity and gradual change that never disturbs the travelling soul. Its journey has become harder – gradually – and more painful, but it has been prepared.

Consider – does anything on your earth lead you to think that the body of a plant or animal could be put back together once it has decayed? Does anything in the nature of your whole world do that? NO! It moves forward into the next generation, is propagated and repeats the life-form again in a new body. Never, NEVER the old one

rehashed, put back together. The law of your earth is set –
birth, life, death – repeated by the next generation of
bodies. What can be repeated is a soul incarnating in
another of these repeated bodies.

Now, thinking modern woman and man, does this not
make sense? A glove appears animated by the fingers
within. You wear a glove until it is unfit to be used
because it is worn and tattered, when you would cast it
away and put on another new glove. You would move
your fingers and again apparently animate the piece of
clothing. So do you move on to a new body in the fullness
of time, after the death of your last.

Imagine a soul has come to the end of its days in a
human form; quietly it passes out of the body in the
manner I have previously described. It is a little weak
from the last illness but more so from the fact that it has
been used to being weak and continues to think it is still
suffering from weakness. People appear to come and look
after it, sometimes they are people it knew in its earthly
life, loved ones. It dawns on it that something has
happened, changed. Gradually it learns that it has left the
earthly body behind and that it is inhabiting an
apparently new body.

This is a scenario that happens over and over again. It
is a picture of the majority of earthly leavings of the body
by the soul and the start of residence in the etheric regions.
There are a million other scenarios but each is less
frequent than the above.

This is because the majority of people die when their
normal time has come in old age, and most are of a mental
and spiritual development that takes them to a similar
level of post-physical life. I will have a lot more to say later
about these mental and spiritual connotations having a

bearing on our post-physical life. Yet I will say just a few words now, for your minds will probably be jumping to thoughts of 'terrible judgements' on the life just past. At the moment the etheric body comes out of the physical body there is no one and nothing to pass any judgement on its performance during its life on earth.

There is no one who can take away its soul or tell it where to go. There are however nearly always plenty of other souls there to help and comfort the newly dead soul, explain whatever is necessary and suggest that it comes with them to a place of rest and recuperation.

But although there is no judgement by another soul, however highly placed or sponsored, there is a determination of the quality of help and place to which the soul may go made entirely by that soul itself!

Who knows you better than you? Who knows the truth, the very truth about you, better than you? Who is fitter to judge (if you must have that word), judge you better than you yourself? Nobody in your universe nor even in the Spiritual Universe.

And so it is. You decide for yourself, and in the dimensions you are about to enter can do nothing else, for you have left the physical that hid so much, both good and bad, behind. Here in the etheric we are seen for what we are and we can no longer hide it.

As I have said, the vast majority are in what might be termed a middling state, often more sinned against than sinning themselves, that is if we take 'SIN' to mean an action of wrong. Oddly, it is not the deeds themselves that are so important but the moral issue behind their perpetration. Not even that, but one step removed, the thinking behind the morals and the general development in the soul's consciousness that the deeds were wrong. It is this development that matters. If the soul has developed enough to know the wrong it does, this will have its effect in its post-physical life. How does that happen? I will try and explain, for the reason is practical not theological.

The afterlife in the etheric dimensions has been covered many times in what is termed Spiritualist literature. There have been many books describing what is variously called the Summerland, the spheres (not our spheres of the Spiritual Universe), and the etheric worlds. And very good most of them are. I refer the reader to almost any of them. There they will find a plethora of detail and explanations of the afterlife. Because this book is being written with a different purpose in mind I am not going to give you long details here of what you will find in these worlds. I leave you, my reader, to do some research elsewhere into nitty gritty details of after physical death existences. Here we are going to concentrate on basic details and then take them further.

We have talked about the Etheric sphere before in pre-physical life and in between physical life. I mentioned that the rings in our symbol that represent the pre and post-physical spheres touch, symbolising that one is composed of the same material as the other. It is all one pervasive, interpenetrating sphere operating on the etheric wavelengths. In it, the physical sphere has its being. One is the basis of the other. In truth the etheric rings represent one sphere not two.

Beings, souls, who have entered this universe from the Angelic regions and taken up their abode here can move about their particular wavelength of the etheric as they wish. According to their development, their stage of their journey, they can go elsewhere in the etheric. How? One, as they move downwards on the scale of the etheric which they do by taking various lives in each level, as we have discussed; and two, with knowledge, experience and wisdom they can change their present revolutions of their make-up to coincide with another and manifest on that level. This changing is done quite scientifically but needs great experience and knowledge. It is also accomplished by thought.

I have mentioned this before and it is something that must be understood to make sense of the worlds etheric. They are malleable to thought, can be moved, changed, made, ended by a thought. Now I do not mean a thought like a misty wraith that sometimes passes for thought on your world. I mean a conscious, formed, concentrated and actual thought in precise detail, in such detail that if you had such a thought you would have to commit it to paper or more likely, as this book is, to computer, word by word, drawing by drawing, line by line.

Of course not all human thoughts are thin and insubstantial. Some are strongly held, locked up in the character and persona of the human. These thoughts could range from absolute knowledge of electronics or some other science to views about politics, ethics or a strongly held religious belief. Although these thoughts have no outward sign other than the behaviour of the thinker, in the etheric they have form and reality. Yes, the very thoughts you now hold are in the etheric, in real form. Have I not said, you are even now etheric in construction as well as physical?

What happens is the same thing that has happened ever since the total soul's beginning when it drew energy from that eternal spark of the Great Spirit. That eternal spark is a creative force, the creative force of the Spiritual Universe, and it is still yours, you have not left it behind.

I know it was split but it is still the same spark of divinity, shared out with your sister soul-cells and later yet again with your brother souls. That mind-love-power could always form things and bodies out of constituent parts, you have always been able to do this. Then, in the physical you chose a life-form that was very heavy and not malleable to thought once you were encased in it. You suspended your ability in your physical form. But unconsciously, in the etheric, when you think, you can still make or create a thought form which you will be able see when you no longer live in the physical.

Here is an interesting thought that might make it clearer to you. The artist must think of the picture before he paints it with pigments and on surfaces that are physical. He will think very hard and fight to get a true likeness of that thought down on his canvas or paper. But sadly it will never be as good as his thought picture. It is something that has driven many an artist to despair, not understanding that what he wanted to create was an impossibility in his physical world. But one day, when he views things with his etheric eyes, after death, he will see his 'original picture' created with his etheric mind and, in all likelihood, he will gasp at the beauty he has created.

How lovely. What a lovely idea. But what about those whose thoughts have not been so well constructed, whose thoughts were anything but beautiful, nice, indeed were totally disgusting? What indeed? There, to use the Bard's words, *'is the rub'*. For not only is the residue of practical thoughts waiting, but also the results of moral, ethical and spiritual thoughts. These last do not so much take an actual form as have a result on the immediate surroundings of the soul. There are some results that transform themselves into almost a symbolic form, like a good and conscientious homemaker will find a home waiting of just the kind they had always dreamed of having, if that is what they want. Or someone who has laboured mightily to relieve the needs of human beings, nursed them, comforted them, loved them, will find that quality returned in equal measure and much more.

But here, there is a great difference from your world where all operate on the same wavelength regardless of character, wealth or status. Here, in the etheric, we are what we are, no more and no less. And at first we can only operate in the waveband to which we belong. This band is akin to light. But the power for that light is the soul's gathered total character-development-spirituality. It is related to the knowledge-wisdom-love that it has been seeking in the physical. Upon release back into the etheric levels it can be seen at a glance, the richness or poverty of this resource, by the light the soul radiates from its very being. This 'light' is the amount of love-force that the soul has managed to bring through from its centre and manifest. Yes, the very fuel which it has sought.

After the first few lives this light is extremely dim, almost non-existent, and it is the reason why the soul has to return to the physical as many times as is necessary to learn to bring that love-force through the layers of its being. It needs the adversity of the physical lives to be able to accomplish this. Each time it leaves an earthly body the soul will judge itself by the mere fact that it will find itself at its own level.

This level is determined by the place on the scale of revolutions, the vibrational rate of the etheric material of the soul's etheric body. This is quite complicated to explain but I will try my best.

The soul has taken on denser and denser etheric

material to be at the stage to manifest on the physical. While experiencing the physical, mineral, vegetable and animal, the etheric body that interpenetrated the physical was composed of this dense etheric matter. Then the soul reaches the stage of turning the corner and starting towards home. To do this it is going to have to make the journey in reverse.

Obvious really, isn't it? It has put on coats and coats of denser and denser material, hidden its core of love under so many particles to gain experience. Now, if it wishes to return, and it does, it is going to have to lose every one of those particles again. It does this almost as slowly as it gained them!

The first stage of this journey is to take on a life that although it is still physical, is of a higher level. I mean as a human, a homo sapiens or some other species elsewhere in other universes of the physical level. Here the soul has a chance to inhabit a body that has the greater mental powers which it is going to need. It is the very first stage in its return to the mental being it once was, but a stage so far removed that it can hardly be recognised as such. Yet that is what it is. The journey so far has been almost totally directed towards being, sensing, experiencing. It has manifested as things and lower forms of beings. It has been learning the practical science of existence. Of course it learnt other things along the way but these practical matters have been foremost in its reason for existence. In truth it will have had little time for anything else for these things take up a great deal of energy and time. Just fighting for existence, the right to have this or that life, for there are many others only too willing to snatch it away for themselves, leaving the first soul to find another. Yes, it is very much like that when it comes to finding a human body in which to incarnate.

This is an important fact. So often the cry is heard, 'I didn't ask to be born'. This is not true. It is so far from the truth as to be laughable. Let me make this very plain. You not only wanted to be born but fought for the right to have the body in which you now find yourself. You did it by dint of asserting yourself and your right. Now this is where the law of cause and effect can really be seen to be working.

If you have caused the right circumstances then the effect will follow. That effect may be that you have enough will-power and strength of character to win the right to a certain body, and it is greater than any other soul's right. It is not easy. You can't just decide it's time for another life and pick out who you would like to be. Cause and effect will dictate the choice as will other laws that govern these things, natural laws of the Great Spirit, not statutes of law like your man-made laws.

While waiting for that moment, all souls will try again and again to take possession of a new body that they hope they can use. There is a huddle of souls waiting around a likely conception, of any kind, even a test tube conception. If there is the possibility that it will produce a vehicle then that is enough. It does not matter where the conception takes place, the method of the soul's inducing of life in those cells is the same. It interpenetrates it and uses the body.

Much like the strongest sperm will be the one to penetrate the ova, beating millions of others to the chance to be the one to fertilise the egg, the soul that is strongest-willed will win out against the other competing souls. If it was not determined enough, positively wanting it with every particle of its being, it would not get it.

This is especially true of earlier human level

incarnations. The soul will try to be the incarnator of any body that it can. But as the soul has its lives in this form it develops. It looks for bodies that will allow it to fulfil its needs and desires. It will desire to live in bodies that are going to have the sort of life the soul wants. If anything this will make the competition stronger in intent but not in numbers. This latter presupposes that the incoming soul has access to knowledge of the future. This, in a way, is true.

At first it is not really the soul that knows where to get this information, especially younger souls. It is its guides that have this knowledge. You see at this stage of the journey the soul will receive much guidance and advice. Each will have a soul or souls who are interested in its development. Why particularly now? Well the soul is at last capable of being one who could make the return journey home with that necessary fuel. It must be encouraged to do this.

So where do the guides get the knowledge of the future and what the life might hold in store for any particular body? They get it from what are called on your world the 'Akashic Records'. No, not a myth, but often misinterpreted into one like 'The Book of Judgement' wherein all names and their deeds are thought to be inscribed.

Now 'Records' usually means a keeping of facts that have happened. This is true of the Akashic Records. In them is found a record of all that happens, every tiny fact. But there is also a way of using these records to see the future possibilities. This is done by using the law of cause and effect. If there is a fact, a cause, an effect can be estimated. In your present society this should not seem too improbable. With your computers, if you give them all the details you can on any subject, the computer can be asked to predict what will happen, what will be the outcome of certain actions. To be honest, the Akashic Records are much better at it than your computers and any soul able to consult them has a pretty good chance of a correct prediction.

When a likely body is about to come into existence which is to be of the right kind with the right experiences likely to happen to it, the guide of a soul will know and advise that soul of its imminence. If it is the right one for the soul, that will be the one who gains control; if it is not, it will fail. Another body will have to be sought. The soul will have to wait, sometimes for hundreds of your earth years. So you see, you were very pleased to incarnate; you may have been waiting a long time for your chance. Do not be fooled by thinking, 'Look at all the humans there are, it can't be too hard to find a body'. There are many many times more souls looking for incarnations than there are human bodies available. This is why I say they will take any chance, any chance of obtaining a human body.

Do things ever go wrong? Does the body go to the wrong soul? Yes and no. Sometimes the sheer overwhelming force of another soul will conquer the one for whom the body would have been perfect. Yet if it is conquered then it was not ready for that body and it will probably be better for that soul to find another in the long run. It is sad but we do not get everything we would like to have, even in the etheric. But there is always another and another chance, chances without end, and time is of no importance in eternity.

The moral dimensions, which are also important in the choice of a new life, will be gone into later. In practice, the soul will attain its desire for incarnations according to its needs and these will be as few or as many as are needed.

In between it will reside in the etheric dimensions just outside the physical. So where are these worlds? There are two answers to this question.

Around any physical world there are layers of etheric matter which coalesce into forms, places, levels of existence which can be used by the soul as a place to live. They look much like the physical world. They are composed of souls in between physical incarnations, both pre-human and post-human. The basic mineral is formed of souls whose next mineral existence will be physical, a pre-physical try out. The vegetation is composed of the souls that are resting between incarnations. Do you remember I said they went back and kept their last form until the next incarnation? This is where they do it. When the souls reach the animal stage they also return to these levels and become the resident fauna of these levels.

Yes, this is why you will see your pets again should you wish to do so, or should they wish to see you. I am sure there are some owners that the pet would never want to clap eyes on again, but there are others that go wild with joy at finding their beloved masters and mistresses again.

And to these lands go humans upon their deaths. These levels around any world are sometimes called the Summerland, the Spheres, the heavenly lands. The name is not important; understanding its constitution is. It is part of the etheric universe and is made up of levels concentric around the physical earth. They are steps down to and back from the physical earth. Each physical universe within the etheric universe has these step down levels of etheric matter becoming denser the nearer to the physical level they get. They are the way the soul makes its final way to the physical level.

These layers, steps, are not literally going up or down,

further or nearer to your earth. They are interpenetrating levels. In truth they are existing exactly where you are existing, all of them. From the finest, highest, right down to your level, for do you not see, really you live on the very densest etheric level. But it is so dense it is called the physical sphere, thought of as a separate sphere. It can only be used by the method I have described whereas in all the other etheric levels we manifest by changing the revolutions of the etheric atoms of our being – not by interpenetrating it. This is why the Etheric/Physical Universe is one with the physical within the etheric. The physical is its densest level.

The second answer is that there are other etheric worlds that the soul will incarnate on, prior to and post going to one of these multi-level worlds that lead to and from a physical life. These other etheric worlds are of a much finer nature than any of the levels leading to a physical level, and are worlds in their own right, in their own universes. They are the worlds to which the post-Angelic ones come upon their entry into our particular wheel of creation. These finer worlds will be discussed when we reach that point. For now, you and I have our being on one of the physical worlds or the steps to it. Does it remind you of a vision picture given in earlier times? A symbol? Yes, Jacob's ladder and the Angels going up and down. It was a symbol of the etheric layers.

Perhaps you are now getting some idea of how it can be possible for you to come and go to your world many times. Although I have tried to make you realise that you can have incarnations on other worlds, other universes, it was because I have been engaged in trying to make you open your mind. Now I must modify that information. It is not that it is not true, it is, but it is more usual to choose a certain branch of life and have most of your incarnations in that branch. Once in that universe, that world, it is quite hard to go to others, it takes a lot of energy and is only done when the universe you are in fails, dies, or the kind of the life you need is just not available. Then it is possible to transfer. The move from mineral to vegetation is an example of transfer to another universe; its own no longer exists. It is also possible when a soul reaches a point of change, vegetation to animal – animal to human type. This is usually only a change to another world within its own immediate physical universe.

Once it has embarked on a period of one type of existence it will usually have all its consecutive lives on that world. Hence a soul in its human stage will return to the same earth for all its following experiences of that level of life. It will have grown extremely attached to its world and understand it, long for it and its possibilities. So you will in all probability have had other lives on your very earth. That you do not remember them is not important, for when you relinquish your present body, there will come a time when you will recall them all in detail.

Immediately you die from your present body you will manifest on the level to which you belong in the ladder of etheric dimensions pertaining to your world. It will be regulated by yourself and no one else. It will be the effect of how you lived your life affecting the revolutions of the etheric atoms of your etheric body. This effect has been caused by the amount you have been able to allow your soul to come through the many layers of your make-up. This process of the love-force being brought through the layers actually refines the particles of the etheric body and is the method of determining your new home. That infinite quality of the love-force is what you have been seeking to express. When you have not succeeded, or not enough to make any difference, you would have stayed on the lower levels of the etheric and later tried again. If you come out of a life and find yourself on a higher level, it may be from that time on you no longer have to return to earth. You will put your energy to climbing the ladder out of the environs of this particular world, this particular universe.

There are many levels, many steps to climb. It takes a long while. I am still on the ladder and in all likelihood will be for a long time yet. But sooner or later I will reach the level where I will escape from the etheric levels about the earth and progress to those finer worlds for a series of lives. There I gather I will refine away more of my dross etheric atoms by learning to express even more of my soul, my love-force. In truth I am beginning to long for this; I no longer wish to stay in the earthly etheric levels and long for this change, a longing which is natural. It is a wish that is the propelling force, the driving force to make me take the difficult steps homewards. It is the deep yearning of which I have spoken before. But now I begin to understand this yearning. Where the law of deepening density made the soul move downwards through spheres, the yearning within the soul for its home pulls it back up through the spheres.

Chapter 8

The Group Soul

As the time comes to end our series of earthly lives, so there will be a moment to end our total life in our multi-level Etheric/Physical world. We come out of that last human life at whatever level we choose. It must of necessity be of a certain grade of fineness or the decision not to have further physical lives would not be possible. From that point on we live and learn in those etheric dimensions spoken of in the previous chapter. Learn to express more of that light, that love-force. It is as if we are turning ourselves inside out. Not literally, but no longer hiding our light. As this happens the etheric atoms of the etheric body refine, operate on faster levels, different levels, wavelengths. And so you see those new levels, perceive them and the denizens of those levels see you.

In practical terms, then, a soul now passes up the ladder or through the varying etheric levels, sojourning as long or wherever suits its needs. I personally live in just such a realm. To visit you I have had to change the revolution rates of my make-up and consciously make myself visible to the lower, denser levels nearer your earth. I have not made myself dense enough for physical beings to see me for, as I have explained, that has to be done by the different method of an interpenetrating incarnation. I did not come to have another physical life. I remained outside the physical to do the work necessary in order to pass these words through the veil. I and the rest of our group. You might now ask to what group do I refer, is it anything to do with the pre-physical soul group? Oh yes, indeed it is.

Our group is made up mostly of members of the soul-cell that broke up into its individual souls as it entered into physical existence. For although we separated and passed our own ways the link between us was never broken. Nor is the link you have with your brother souls. But by the time you have gone through all your physical and particularly your human type lives you can no longer see that link. You can, however, feel it. Somehow that sense is never lost. Among millions and millions of souls from other groups, the soul will sense, feel, be drawn to a member of its own group, should it chance upon it. In human terms they may become deep friends, lovers, or even man and wife. The love between them will be instinctive and long lasting. Is this then the answer to what the world call soul-mates? Yes and no. When you meet any member of your group you will love them. You will not be able to help yourself, and it will take whatever form of love seems suitable, for all love is the same. If circumstances separate you, you will feel sadness, pain and grief.

There are other factors to consider before we look at 'soul-mates'. First, there are all the other souls we meet and find attractive, yet do not always continue to desire or even need. The explanation is often that they come from another soul-cell that belongs to your total soul-group. They too are making the journey through the physical and quite often become partners or friends while in physical incarnation with a member of another fellow soul-cell. As to the rest of our relationships, they are with what might be termed outsiders. It is actually these relationships which develop our souls more because, of necessity, there will be friction and trouble, pain from which we learn and progress. Look about you as you move through your world and study people's relationships. You will soon be able to see what I am talking about. The couple that are so similar stay together through thick and thin, cannot live without each other. *'What do they see in her or him?'* you sometimes hear people say. He or she hasn't seen, but they have felt.

This grouping then is a factor behind much of human interaction which is not known or taken into consideration. For instance, you might meet a member of a group who has been an enemy of your group over aeons of time and wonder at their venom when you have done nothing to occasion it. Yes, it works in the negative as much as in the positive. It is this side of the journey we will look at later. For now, know that your soul-group is very important. You have individualised and gained knowledge of your inner self, your inner spark of divinity. As you start to reach out towards the source of that divinity and find you wish to achieve reunion with that divinity, you are going to have to learn to sublimate self, that very individuality that you have gained. It is not exactly sublimation but rather a joining, and the first step is taken with your soul-mate.

As the soul-cell breaks down and the souls loosen to
become individual, the breakdown is accomplished in
stages. First a half, quarter, and eighth of the total number
will cling together. This goes on until there are only two
souls, twin souls. They relate very closely to each other
and although the same in many ways they each have some
attributes that the other does not have. When they
eventually break apart in the final parting they will feel
that something is missing. It is. It is seeking for that which
is missing which will drive the soul to undertake
vicissitudes it never dreamed possible.

You see, although a soul may meet its twin in the
etheric between lives, it is not always the moment of
absolute recognition of each other. Of course they sense an
enormous attraction for each other and often dive into a
physical life that they hope will run parallel, where they
will meet and be joined in a relationship. Mother, father,
siblings, lovers, friends. But once in the flesh it doesn't
always work out. One may have a body that does not
survive beyond infancy. The other looks in vain for its
mate and has to make do with whatever love and
affection, relationships it can find. It often is thought that
the soul-mate has been found when it has not. These
relationships will be with other soul-cell members and be
almost as strong as with the soul-mate. But somewhere,
sometime, in the physical or the etheric, the soul will have
to admit this is not 'The One'.

There will, of course, be times when the soul will meet
its soul-mate in a physical incarnation and they know
each other in an earthly relationship. These meetings are
what cause the greatest of love stories in your world, the
greatest of friendships, the greatest of sacrifices. Do not
think all these meetings on earth or in the earthly etheric

regions are all man-woman relationship, lovers. It could be parents and children, siblings, two friends of the same sex, any combination of two people. These meetings are not all known or world shattering, but whenever it happens it causes a great light to shine. The joy of finding the beloved.

It happens in a lesser way every time a soul finds one of its group but never in the way it does when soul-mates reunite. Even this reunion is not complete. It only means they are together in individual form. The finding of each other is important but the recognition that this is the one is even more important. Meanwhile, love prevails.

Nor does that recognition mean that these reunited soul-mates are going to merge into one immediately they find one another. Very unlikely indeed. More than likely they still both have a long way to go in learning the meaning of life and existence. Sometimes they go on together incarnating nearby and sometimes they become quite separated again.

Eventually they will come together in a form that means they will remain together. It will be a point where one has personified as a man and the other as a woman. It matters not which way they choose. It will fall out naturally. Somewhere one life has usually been spent together as physical mates but it may not be the last life before quitting earthly incarnations. It is often in the form where they were physical mates that twin souls come together.

Soul twins may be on completely different levels of development. One may progress to the point of no return to earth and begin its journey up the etheric ladder of dimensions, the other still held in the slough of physical existences. The one who has developed will know where its mate is and will wait on some suitable level until the other can join it. That may seem unfair as one is holding the other back from progressing. There are much longer waits in store and it is rare for a twin soul to be too far behind or in front. But the less advanced soul has to find the higher levels by its own efforts and lessons, although the higher soul of the two will advise and give comfort wherever it can. But it cannot do that soul's work for it, suffer its vicissitudes or stop in any way the results of the law of cause and effect.

If you have a longing to find that special person which is so strong you feel almost ill with despair and longing, it will mean that at last you have come to the point where you begin to understand the need to be part of someone else. In all probability you will soon find your own soul-mate, but by *soon* I don't mean it will be in your present physical life. Maybe the loved one is waiting just beyond death, knowing that this time you will stay together. As I said, it will be a man and woman, and at first their joining will be as lovers. I do not say as husband and wife although this can be the case if the last incarnation was in this form. But lovers, the loved and the beloved. Love in every form more beautiful than you can ever imagine. Joy, passion, enjoyment, togetherness, everything you would expect of true love.

What of other loves, your last physical mate who may have loved you very dearly and needed you? Well, by the time this joining of soul-mates happens all these things will be sorted out and understood by all. The soul-mates are free of every other relationship and can come together in a higher level for what amounts to a spiritual marriage. Nobody is given and no one taken. It is absolutely equal. No words are said and no contracts or promises made. It is just obvious to the pair and to everyone else. For as I have said, things are not hidden from us in these realms. Soul-mates who have recognised each other just do not want to be paired with any other soul ever again.

From then on the pair work and learn together. They may separate at times to visit some special place or use their particular knowledge where it is needed, but on the whole their path will be the same. They will join in the same projects, plans, work. Oh, we have plenty of that. Did you think you would do nothing for ever and ever? Not so, this book is just such a project.

After whatever time the two souls required to make the journey to the highest, finest level on the earthly etheric regions, they would be so close as to almost seem to be one. This is exactly what is happening, for now we have to remember, re-learn, how to merge and become part of a whole, something that is accomplished by love. For if you love another greatly you wish to be at one with them. Taken at its lowest level this is the love between two souls who have a history that stretches back to the time they left the great source. Taken at this level it is a love between a man and a woman, human souls.

One day the pair will reach a point that they leave the confines of the etheric regions connected with earth and will move to having lives on a series of finer etheric worlds, worlds sufficient unto themselves, and leading to a refining of the spiritual nature of the souls, as well as the actual etheric body. The two things are related in that as the soul becomes more spiritual in outlook its body will become more able to express itself in worlds of finer and finer quality. For with spiritualization comes knowledge and wisdom to be able to manipulate the fine ethers of these worlds.

Lives are chosen and lived for as long as it is necessary, lives that are lived on worlds that are composed of the expressions of those making the journey in the reverse direction. Yes, the worlds these post-human souls live on are made up of the incarnations of those who have come from the Angelic realms. This is why the two spheres are one in reality, the difference being that the pre-human souls have not as yet had a human incarnation, so they cannot manifest as such. Those making the upward journey will always manifest as human souls and, at this time, will still have an outwardly human appearance. There is however great communion between the two, the upward moving soul and those descending. Great love and respect, help and mutual assistance pass between them. For one is not needed to sustain the other as in the earthly regions; only one gives substance to the other's world. One is not consumed by the other, only used as malleable material to create what is needed.

This is because by this time the 'Body' of the human soul does not need sustenance nor does it have eliminations. It is sustained by what it breathes which does not require the substance it uses to die, only change its form, something all minerals can do without giving up their incarnation. This breathing has to be done almost consciously and it was learnt – guess where? Of course, on the physical world in which you live.

So peace and harmony reign between the environment and the peoples of these worlds. These are the worlds I now long to see and reside upon but my time has not yet come. It will and when it does I shall no longer be able to return to these earthly etheric regions in my present form. I will be able to impinge upon them, by thought, visit in such a way that it will seem to those there that I am with them but I will not be there in truth. Only a thought form of myself, which can be any shape I please, though it is usual to assume the likeness those left behind remember. It is a death of a sort but you leave behind no body, for you have merely transformed the one you had to a higher frequency which has put you out of touch with your former vibrations. Other changes ensue and you cannot return as before.

But the soul very rarely wants to return, for the time has come to progress. There are those who are the masters and teachers, guides and helpers who return by the method I have described. They come to teach us on these levels in which I have my residence in much the same way as, may I say in all humility and love, I come to teach you. I want to come to you; it is my delight and also for the necessity of my own soul that I come to you. So also do these great souls from the higher etheric worlds come to us and show us the way forward. It is from them I learn what I must pass on to you and how to do it. They give me constant guidance and upliftment when things do not progress as I would have them do. They counsel patience when I fume at the difficulties, and give praise when I succeed in the smallest trifle. Always they come manifesting with a love so great that it is hard to bear. They are most wondrous, yet they are still of our Etheric/Physical Universe. They will not be for much longer, for they are souls on the upward journey and they are near to what has been termed the second death.

Upon the highest level of the Etheric/Physical Universe, the soul comes to the borders of its confines. There is a place where the Etheric/Physical Universe ends. It is more the dimension that changes at this point which marks the borders of the Etheric with the Angelic, yes, the very Angelic realms that we passed through on our downward journey. You see, if we take our symbol of the seven spheres and gently squeeze them together can you see what happens?

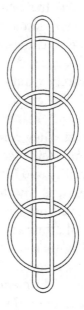

Obvious really. Each sphere lies within the other and it is done in the same way as I have just explained. Those incarnating on the downward journey are the worlds and the flora and fauna of those worlds. They are peopled by the souls of those on the upward journey. There are some places where there are only those on the downward journey and possibly places where there are those who are on the upward who can reside without recourse to substance.

The time comes when, as I yearn to leave behind the earthly etheric regions, and you possibly yearn never to return to the physical realm, the time comes when the soul yearns to return to the Angelic regions. Remember these regions are composed of energy particles. This means that the soul will have to cast aside every last vestige of etheric matter to enter into these sublime regions. When it does, its life in the Etheric/Physical Universe is over. It will never return in a form of which the inhabitants of that universe would be fully cognisant. Again it can impinge upon those left behind but it cannot return to take up another form or life there. It will now progress and have its being in the Angelic or energy realms.

Before this can take place there is much that must happen to a soul. From the moment it moves out of the earthly environs it is no longer 'A' soul but will have been reunited with its twin. Slowly in the etheric worlds they learn to operate as one. Loneliness is something these souls never know again. Gradually they will realise that their hearts beat as one, their thoughts are as one and their will is as one. They will have had many experiences together and the love binding them is unbreakable, unshakeable. As two they have more power, more ability, more knowledge and wisdom. Eventually they will want to be one and this wanting will cause it to happen. They will merge and appear as one.

There has been something else happening during all this time since leaving the last earthly sojourn and the highest level of the etheric worlds. Not only has the soul sought and found its soul-mate, it will find that it has re-gathered with others to live among original soul-cell members. Many it will recognise as those who have been relations and friends in many lives; those it could not understand why they held such a great attraction, sometimes making them do anything to be able to express their love. This is sometimes the explanation of a same sex love affair or incestuous love. The drive of another soul being of the same soul-cell is enormous. Many things become understandable once this fact is realised. It could be called a spiritual instinct. It is something that no one can ignore. On your world it can only be felt, but in later states it can literally be seen. It is more than family resemblance; members of a soul-cell are different facets of the same being.

You will recall that the total soul broke up into its constituent soul-cells as it crossed into the Etheric/ Physical Universe and the soul-cells broke down into individual souls as they entered the physical. You may think that exactly the reverse would happen as the soul took the journey in reverse but this is not quite so. When the soul is once again on these borders it will pass into the etheric earthly realms as a single soul and remain so for some time. Then, as a duo it re-gathers with its soul-cell members on the borders of the Etheric/Physical Universe.

Then begins the long wait. As I have said, it can be a long wait until the soul finds its soul-mate; it is nothing to the wait some souls have for all their group to gather. Some may be left far behind, still caught in the toils of physical incarnation. For you see, not one member of the soul-cell can cross the border, pass onwards without *all* its sister soul-cell mates being ready to do so as well.

Not only must they be there but time must have been taken for them to become, once more, a cohesive group, not one more important than another. This then is the problem and the work that must be done on the etheric worlds leading upwards to the light of the Angelic realms. The union of the twin souls must be consolidated and together they must learn to work, once again, with members of their group.

Sometimes a group, a soul-cell, will start to congregate even before moving to the finer etheric worlds, as it is in my own group. But not all are here. Some are way behind, some are in front, so to speak. It is not necessary that they all be gathered before any one member can move onward, only that the soul-mate be found and present.

Well, that is as it seems to be for the vast majority of souls. There always seem to be those few exceptions, those paradoxes that abound in the Great Spirit's universes. Not exactly outside the Great Spirit's infinite laws but operating the laws with greater knowledge. We could operate under them in the same way also, if only we knew how. But even the great ones must conform to laws that are totally universal.

So barring a few exceptions we human souls have found and enjoyed the company of our twin soul for some little time, are beginning to think and feel as one when we pass from the earthly etheric dimensions to the finer etheric worlds. There we join more closely and work together to bring about a regrouping of the soul-cell. No soul loses any part of itself and indeed it gains a great deal. After much searching and consolidating, the group will have come together, each with his or her twin, going through the process of merging.

Among these twins, each re-joined pair of souls will find another pair of twins that attracts them. There will be something special about these twins that causes them to feel love of a stronger nature than for the others of the group. When the time comes to move onwards it will probably be in the company of this other pair of twin souls forming a foursome, helping each other, giving support and comfort in their new form of existence. For they have all been losing touch with the etheric particle and beginning to use their energy forms. As in the downward journey, at the moment they no longer hold any etheric particles within their make-up, they cease to operate in that universe and have their being in the Angelic realms once more.

Does this mean they have become Angels? Not exactly. They have become of such a beauteous and fine quality that they have won the right to live in those hallowed realms. Is this then heaven? Yes and No. It is heavenly but with there being so many wonderful, heavenly realms, who can say which is heaven? Heaven to one may not be quite heaven to another. In truth it is but a realm that we, the journeying soul, pass through and in which we have our being while there.

That the souls that reside there are far beyond our conception of what is good, holy, pure, wise, kind and loving, in fact they personify as love to us, is true. If this is what you think of as an Angel, then these are now Angelic ones. I somehow doubt that they think of themselves as that. For their new form will allow them to begin to experience the distant heat of the centre of the fire. They will begin to have direct experience, however infinitesimal in the first instance, direct experience of the Great Spirit and they realise how far they have yet to go. Do you recall I said of these realms, on the downward sweep of our journey, that they are the 'Ante-room' to the Great Spirit's Presence?

The joy that must be felt is unimaginable to us poor mortals and ex-mortals. Try to feel. The soul has the joy of being with its loved one, so closely together they are one. They, together, have re-found all their sister souls and among them will be one re-joined pair that have become very dear and close to them. Together the group has completed great feats, done great works. Each one has overcome every Etheric/Physical difficulty and danger. Combined, they have enormous reservoirs of knowledge and experience, terrific power to control their environment and most of all, they have learnt about the fuel of love that they came to gather. They have collected it and found how to transport it and themselves towards their destination, their source. The energy of love now enfolds them and they are welcomed to their new sphere, as they were once welcomed by loved ones as they left the earth on their various deaths.

This then is the second death if you wish to call it that. It only happens once and it only happens when all the members of your soul-cell are quite ready and willing for it to happen. There is no return of the soul to the Etheric/Physical Universe again, although, as before, an impingement can be made by the use of thought.

What the lives of these beings is like is hard to imagine, for they are now operating entirely within the spheres comprised of energy particles. It is thought that a semblance is kept of the human they once were and when they impinge by thought transference on those left behind, they certainly send a mind-picture of that form.

But recall, the Etheric/Physical Universe was only one of any number of universes the total souls could choose to live within. This then means that there will be souls in the Angelic spheres that have been sojourning in other universes and will be returning in a like manner with the fuel they have gathered. They will be of an equal nature to our returning human souls but they will not be human souls. They will be whatever the equivalent is that their universe produces. Of course there will be the wonder of discovering all these different forms of soul life and they will be able to communicate – by thought. Indeed that is the key to these realms. Thought will be more important than form.

I therefore feel, and have been given to understand, that as the soul resides in that unimaginable sphere, there will be a gradual loss of keeping to any particular form as thought contact becomes paramount. However, I am also assured that the basic fact of the form gained in whatever the physical or physical counterpart is, will be retained forever. This is the container of the fuel; the fact that makes each universe produce its own particular fuel.

The first period of existence in this sphere will be used to consolidate the soul-cell. Although all the members of the soul-cell move back into the Angelic realms together, not all the soul-cells of any one total soul will be present. There will probably be some nearby who have kept station with brother soul-cells but it is unlikely that all will be there. Some may be ahead and some still within the Etheric/Physical Universe.

I am sure you will have guessed that the total souls journeying downwards and personifying in the Angelic realms are the energy worlds of that sphere, the worlds and everything that goes into their make-up. The newly arrived soul-cell containing our pairs of twinned souls, who are already moving towards a second joining, advance into and occupy these Angelic worlds. Together with this other beloved pair, they choose to experience lives on these worlds. These worlds and lives are in a dimension we cannot even begin to imagine.

You will probably feel something as strong as repugnance to the idea of joining, merging with any other being. That is as it should be in your present state. The change to the state of wishing to merge with others is so

far removed from your own that it need be of no
consequence to you except – except to explain what seems
an inexplicable urge to seek the beloved, the other half of
oneself, the soul-mate. Even after finding that mate, the
joining together is so far away, with so much to be
accomplished and understood, with so many changes to
the soul before it happens, as to be ludicrous for those still
on earth to totally comprehend.

But I have come to give you a new outlook, broaden
your horizons. I therefore tell you about these things in a
general way so that you may begin to have knowledge of
them. Maybe in another age, if man progresses enough, he
may begin to understand. There may be those among you
even now who can sense that one might have to lose
oneself to gain something even greater. It has been
propounded by the great teachers. For those great souls
passing along the journey of the soul never quite lose sight
of these matters. They yearn more strongly than others in
every existence to return to where they will lose self to
gain a greater prize. Their teachings therefore reflect this,
and so you have this reflection in the history of your
world that loss of self is to be desired. Yet you find it
difficult to understand, a desire most of you do not have.
This, then, is what the soul is taught on the upward
journey. Gently, slowly, the truth becomes more apparent,
that the individuality gained by such hardship has to be
surrendered, willingly, for the benefit of all, including
oneself.

Chapter 9

The Great Spirit and the Logos

We now enter the penultimate stage of the journey from the outermost edges of the ante-room to the Great Spirit, to the entrance of the presence of the Great Spirit Itself. And from now on my task is almost impossible for how does one describe the indescribable? And where, many of you will be saying, does The Christ come into all this? Does It come into it at all? Indeed It does, but I have purposely left that until the last few chapters where I can give full space to the most important soul in our Etheric/Physical Universe. We have been discussing the practical points of the journey and I will continue in like vein for just a little longer.

The twinned souls, together with the other members of the soul-cell, have crossed the border and now live within the Angelic Realms as a group. The numbers of this group, of course, will vary as to whether it was an old or new total soul originally. There could be thousands, even millions, in the group of a young soul, or as few as two. If it were one of the rarest, a complete soul that never broke down, there would be only one. These latter are so rare that few have ever seen them.

Most groups on earth are in the region of 16 upwards, always in the numerical possibility of division by two or four or eight. From 16 they then continue to double so the next number is 32 and the next 64 and so on. As your world has progressed, become more intelligent, it has attracted more of the smaller numbered souls rather than the larger. But there are still some very large numbered souls passing through. Yes, it is some measure of the age of the original total soul, how many times it has made the great journey. As I have said, it is thought that each soul in the smaller groups is a merged soul, that is, made up of many of the souls that went out from the Great Spirit in the very first instance, on their first journey. So originally, it too would have been a soul of vast numbers. One day the vast numbered soul now passing through the journey will too have merged some of its souls, and on its next journey be a soul of smaller numbers and greater knowledge.

Whatever the numbers of the soul regrouping after its etheric travails, it now has much left to do. At first each two will become more engrossed in another pair, in much the same way as the twin lovers. They will have lives and experiences together, undertake work together and most of all love each other and the other soul-cell members who are about them. Eventually they will be so close as a four that it will be hard to tell them apart. The time will come when they will, of mutual consent, join and be one.

The process will then repeat itself with another four. When it has finished, with another eight. Ah, now you see the mathematics of it.

All the time this is happening the soul-cell has been travelling through the energy realms, moving to finer and finer manifestations. It can do this because of the lessons learnt in the process of losing self, and realising it is gaining more than has been lost. To do this each soul must have infinite love for the others. Each must love the others more than themselves. In doing this they bring forth more of the inner light, the inner source, and as it passes through the layers of accumulated particles, it cleanses and clears them, refines the soul to be able to reside in worlds nearer and nearer the presence of the Great Spirit.

The moment comes when all members of the soul-cell are rejoined and they pass their cognisance back to the whole, complete soul-cell. But not their complete consciousness. They still 'know' themselves. They still interact between themselves but they present a united face to others. I do not know if this united 'face' is human or come to that, if there is a body. I suspect it can have one if it wants to do so.

Here then is a being of magnitude and knowledge, experienced and most loving. The 'Light' that shines forth from one of these beings is inexpressible. It is from these realms that the 'Shining Ones' come. These are what I feel are the Angels of our mythologies. These beings have the knowledge and experience to do so. If they were sent on a mission to the Etheric/Physical Universe and to the human world in particular, I still do not think it would be in actuality. I think it would be accomplished by the usual *modus operandi*, and that is by thought. These merged human souls have such wonderful possibilities they could easily send or broadcast a thought form that would have all the signs of reality to the receiver.

In all likelihood it would personify with much light

and colour round about it, although it could no doubt cut that out if it desired. Now remember the thought form has to be received by the person or a post person and will be subject to their ability to receive correctly and interpret the signal. For that is what it is, just as your radio and television, etc., are signals. What is received is only as good as the apparatus you are using to receive the signal, however modern and up to date it is. A television will not give you coloured pictures if it was only made to receive black and white pictures. Those on earth years ago were schooled to think that Angels had wings, so the lights and colours around the 'vision' appeared as wings. In latter days, mediums have seen and reported only a wonderful light and colour about some beings that they have witnessed. Their ability, their intelligence is improved on their forbears and they are receiving a better picture, a more correct picture.

I have seen these manifestations quite often in our realms. Their coming is always accompanied by great joy and wonder. There are some of us who are lucky enough to have one or two of these beings directly concerned with our progress and learning or involved in and helping our work. Some are almost permanent friends, often coming to visit us, and others come and go as they are needed. There are two or three directly concerned with the writing of this book.

Here then, in the Angelic Realms, resides the complete soul-cell living on worlds composed of the downward journeying total souls. There will have been, or will now be, other soul-cells from the original total soul gathering together with their brother soul-cells. All the same laws apply. Attraction to each other. Love of each other. Recognition of each other. And an exchange of knowledge with each other. In the higher worlds of the Angelic spheres is where, once more, the unit, the soul-cells of the total soul reunite with one another. There now happen processes very much as I have described in the first part of this chapter between the soul-cells, but the numbers concerned are smaller. Of course there is our paradoxical 'One' soul who is still as rare, then two, four and so on, soul-cells making one total soul. It is here that the longest of waits can be experienced in that other member soul-cells may still be far behind. Those soul-cells beginning to rejoin will be at the frontiers of the environs of the mind rather than the energy realm. Most energy particles will have been lost, although some must be retained as long as they remain in the Angelic Realm.

The law now is the same as crossing the frontiers of the etheric into the Angelic. All member soul-cells of any total soul must be present and equal in stature and knowledge, ability and love. All must be in agreement to take the step into the final sphere of the journey of the soul, what we previously termed the Pre-Angelic sphere. It is the same sphere, the sphere of the mind. The sphere where they are in the actual presence of the Great Spirit, welcomed and loved by It directly. This ineffable, unimaginable Spirit is again their companion. I do not see how I can write about this, explain it in such paltry things as human words; I cannot even do it with thought pictures.

The soul-cells that have passed to this sphere will soon join as one in this rarefied atmosphere of love. The skills are now well learnt of how this is done. They will be but on the outer fringes of this sphere yet they will themselves be more wondrous than you and I could possibly picture in our wildest stretches of imagination. It is felt that they progress inwards, if there is an inwards in things of the mind. They will mingle with others until they are at the innermost, nearest point to the Great Spirit without actually being the Great Spirit. They will still have their duties, their works, their responsibilities. For it is through them that the Spiritual Universe operates, is, so to speak, governed.

There come times in this eternity that the Great Spirit has need of replenishment. Parts of Itself have been put forth to renew the whole of creation. If the total soul is ready and willing, having brought with it the fuel gathered by such long and arduous labour while journeying through the Great Spirit spheres, it will have reached its destiny, that which has been written since the beginning of its journey. It will rejoin the Godhead. Once more it will become the Great Spirit Itself.

This then is our final destiny, yours, mine, all souls in every sphere, in every universe, in every world, in every form and state of progression. However positive or negative, good or bad, young or old. Each, in its own way, will one day be, as is said, 'Fit for the table of God.'

Another one of our old friends, a symbol. It does not mean being asked to become a food, a sustenance for the Godhead, it is not giving up one's body or dying a final death or losing consciousness. It is but one more joining, an ultimate joining to actually be that central Love-Power-Energy that runs throughout the whole of the Spiritual Universe. *It is gaining cosmic consciousness.*

*   *   *   *   *

How to proceed from talking about the ultimate and not seem mundane is a difficult problem. This however is what we must now do. Let us imagine we have just been on a round of eternity and have once again been the ultimate ourselves. To be the very Spiritual Universe, imagine, to have cognisance of its uttermost ends, to love everything without exception, to be that awesome Mind-Love-Power. How puny is our imagination for, in very truth, we cannot conceive the Great Spirit. So little can we conceive It that what we think of as God is only a stepping stone to learning how to know the Great Spirit.

Now there is a thought for you. Where in the journey did I speak of another God? I have mentioned It once by name and several times in a form that I said was very, very rare.

It is the Christ Spirit, the Khristös, the Anointed One. It is a total soul that never breaks up into its constituent soul-cells or souls but remains one. Its rarity is because there is but one for each of the universes that adjoin the Angelic Sphere and a few here and there passing through, gaining particular knowledge that they will need on a later journey.

This Etheric/Physical Universe, as all others, has a Christ Spirit into whose charge is given all that pertains to the universes – worlds – realms of that complete universe. It is this Spirit, a Spirit of such magnitude that It is the Great Spirit personified. It's this Spirit that we poor souls imagine is the ultimate. We cannot even really conceive It properly and often have given It the likeness of a mere human. There are some who begin to understand the nature of this Christ Spirit, to conceive that which is of pure energy and mind, but it is still very rare.

This then is the wonder of the Great Spirit's infinite love for all Its creation as we take our downward spiral for Its sake. As we lose sight of the Great Spirit's own self, come out of Its presence, It puts out for us a manifestation of Itself that is suitable to our needs and capabilities. Have I not said that we are never left without the Great Spirit's love and knowledge of our needs?

So we have talked blithely of re-assimilation with the Godhead when we in truth cannot even comprehend properly what might be called the God of our own universe. So where does this Christ Spirit enter into the journey of the Soul? What part does it play in our own journey? Let us set out again on a new round of eternity, another journey of the soul to fetch fuel for the Great Spirit. Some of this journey we will pass through quite quickly and we shall spend time on that which pertains to your present condition and the nearer post conditions of your world.

* * * * *

Again we are the drifting, dreaming Pre-Angelic being, a total soul. According to our lights we choose our path. The right or the left, the positive or the negative. We may be making our choice for the first time as a brash new soul, for it does appear that there are always a percentage of newly created total souls. Perhaps as the older souls amalgamate and merge, several souls are fused into one. New souls are needed to fill the vacuum, the space left. Whatever, it is certain new total souls make their appearance regularly.

The total souls, having decided upon their unalterable path, drift towards the Angelic or energy sphere, there to personify as the worlds upon which we, you and I, will one day reside. There is interaction between these total souls and those using their possibilities. I have not spoken of the interaction between the upward and downward total souls of the Pre-Angelic Realms, for it is not really certain how or if they do interact. It seems probable that they do, as there is communication in the lower spheres, even in our own finer etheric worlds. But I have nothing on which to base a premise that they do. So little is known about what happens in the sphere of the mind, the Pre-Angelic, the sphere of the actual presence of the Great Spirit.

Of the Angelic sphere we know a little more for, as I have said, we receive some visits from the souls there, albeit in thought form, but it appears to us as an actual visit. They teach us a little about their lives, their existences. I must admit it is hard for us to comprehend it entirely.

After the downward travelling total soul has had all the experience it needs in the energy spheres it comes to its second choice – which universe to enter and have its being. What makes it choose a particular universe is not known except in the case of the very old souls, the rarest single total soul or those that comprise the very smallest of numbers in their constituent soul-cells and souls. For these have usually come on a particular mission. Their experience is vast and comprehensive, having travelled through many universes of differing natures.

If the single total soul is making a journey to consolidate its completeness, it may choose to pass through a certain universe for the particular experience of that universe. As I have said, it will be for a future purpose, a purpose we have not mentioned before.

Every now and then a total soul leaves the Great Spirit with the greatest of missions. It will journey in the first instance in just the same way as all the others. It will be watched in awe, for this total soul is the absolute rarest of all. It is a Logos, the Word, a Creator. It has undertaken the most difficult and responsible of all tasks in the search for fuel for the Great Spirit. It has undertaken to create and direct an entire new universe, such as the one in which we reside, the Etheric/Physical Universe, and all its inner universes. Everything of which it comprises is under the direction of such a Spirit. We, of the post physical world in this particular physical universe, have called it the Christ Spirit, or many of us have. By the time you reach the upper earthly etheric realms you may have accepted this name. But some say God, Allah, Jehovah, Zeus, Jove, Brahma, Amen, Aten and oh, so many more.

It does not matter, for really there is no name but rather a presence, an actuality, a *knowing* that needs no name. It is the same for all, whatever language they once spoke on earth, whatever religion they practised or even if they didn't practise one. All come to realise that what they thought of as 'God' is but a stepping stone to the Great Spirit.

But for you of the physical earth I must give It – this wondrous Spirit, our very own personification of the Great Spirit's love for us all – I must give It a name. (Again, the use of It is for literary purposes.) As this book is being written through the mind of a Western woman, it comes more easily to her to use the name most usual in her culture. At first this book will most probably be read by Westerners but should it have the great honour of being translated then perhaps the name most common in that culture should be substituted for the one I will use which is the

THE CHRIST SPIRIT.

I must now demolish any idea you may be having that the religion called 'Christianity' has any supremacy over any other religion in your world. It has not. It has, however, managed to get into its tenets that the Godhead is 'Three in One'. They call it Father, Son and Holy Spirit (or Ghost). This gem of the truth became embedded in a plethora of irrelevant detail often added by those who sought power. But you see the Father represents – is a symbol for – the Great Spirit. The Son represents the Logos, the Word, and the Holy Spirit represents those personifications sent by the Christ Spirit who appear from time to time in earthly incarnations or to do other creative work in the universe.

Now you can see if there are other universes with their own Logos then there is more than one 'Son'. This is so, but not when you are in any one Universe. Only the Logos of your Universe pertains to you, and it is truly through It that you will come to know the Great Spirit. It is through It, 'The Christ Spirit', that every true prayer passes to the Great Spirit.

Now it must be realised that what is thought of as God is the Christ Spirit or Logos. The Great Spirit is even beyond that conception. It is really unconceivable, and is the creator of the Creator. For the Logos is not the ultimate of the Spiritual Universe. It is the Great Spirit who is the One God. Yet still, the Great Spirit is us, the lowest of the low. This is the greatest of the paradoxes of the Spiritual Universe.

So, you must ask next, is the one called Jesus Christ a personification on earth of this Christ Spirit? Yes and no. He pertains to It most definitely, but then so do others such as the obvious ones, Lao Zi, Confucius, Buddha, Mohammed, and in more recent times, the Mahatma Gandhi. There are such souls living on this earth right now as we write this book but they would not thank me for naming them and I will not do so. There will be others yet to come. They are the *'Holy Spirits'*. The ones who show the way, the light, the beloved and closest to our Logos, our Christ Spirit. They are not always teachers or initiators of new religions. As ever, they never pass without being noticed by the world. They may try to hide, become hermits, but the world will find them and both honour and despise them. It cannot be any other way. Who are these spirits? They are those total souls who are very small in number, two or four soul-cells that do not break down into soul units, do you remember? They will have left the Great Spirit at the same time as the Logos, and been attendant upon It, remained with It during Its heroic labours for the Great Spirit.

For understand, these spirits of unbelievable magnitude are subject to all the same laws of the Spiritual Universe as yourself. They are making their journey through the Etheric/Physical Universe just as you are doing but with a particular mission to accomplish. You yourself may be on a lesser mission. All is within the law. They are not 'super spirits', there is no such thing, but they are far greater, superior manifestations of the Great Spirit and that only by their own hand, their own aeons of labour and journeying. How can they not be the beloved of the Logos, Its messengers, Its Holy Spirits? Yet we are all loved by the Christ Spirit in equal measure.

For you see, they are what we can be. The basis of these spirits and even the Logos Itself is of the same make-up as ourselves. That is to say, they have the same 'Flame of Life' within – which is a particle of the Great Spirit – that we have, but they have drawn to themselves such love-knowledge-power that they have become the very signposts, the very gateways to the Great Spirit.

You may be thinking that the soul arriving back at its source would have to be the highest of the most high, but this is not quite the same thing. They are the pure of heart, the carriers of the fuel and magnificent in their own right, but their way home will be pointed out by a Logos.

Although the Logos will remain behind until Its work is done, that is until the end of Its Universe, it is the Logos that is the greater, It and Its Holy Spirits. Only when a total soul is reunited with the Great Spirit, is once more the Great Spirit, will it be greater than the Logos and the Holy Spirits. Within the Great Spirit all is one whatever level the soul was as it returned to the heart of the Spiritual Universe.

Again it might be thought that all total souls merging with the Infinite would be of the absolute height of knowledge and purity. I think the latter is true but remember, some were new young souls and others more experienced as they set out. I think only what is possible is expected of them. The law of there being different levels of progression, standards, still applies even to this final assimilation. Each will have brought what is their offering to the continuation of the whole and it will be found worthy. Do we not shed a tear at the simple gift, from a child, of hastily pulled daisies that are offered so lovingly?

For the likes of you and me as we come to pass through the Gateway of the Logos, it will be as mere grains of cosmic dust almost lost in the unconceivable. Yet it is this that makes me want to weep tears of wonderment, for even that tiny grain is known, loved and cared for. How many times this is proved. We all fit into the plan and the plan is not complete without us and our contribution. That we do not comprehend the plan matters not one whit.

One day, in the history of the Etheric/Physical Universe, will come a time when its use is ended. It is then that the kind of manifestations in 'The Revelations' will come to pass. It may be that your own world will no longer be in existence at that time or it may still be there.

This is not known, nor when this ending will happen. When it does, the Logos will see that all the souls in Its care are on their way home. Then It will gather Its creation to Itself and make Its own return journey to the Great Spirit. It is felt the Christ Spirit will not seek reunion until all that were in Its care have attained their own union with the Ultimate.

How can we have any idea of the magnitude of the task of a Logos? We think our own labours Herculean. Yet through this chain of wondrous souls not one of us is forgotten, not one utterance or deed missed, all are recorded, and their effect, which is always so perfectly apportioned.

Let us now return to the ordinary total soul who, having made the choice of which universe it wishes to make its home, enters it and has its being. Here your own soul, in totality, made its choice of the Etheric/Physical Universe and asked for entrance.

*   *   *   *   *

Asked? Yes, asked, for now you know this Universe is in the charge of our Logos, the Christ Spirit. It is Its permission that is asked and none will enter without it. This Spirit is truly the keeper of the gate. If any are ever refused is not known, but they must want entry with every fibre of their being just as you wanted to incarnate in your particular body. The Christ Spirit can read this for It reads all. Perhaps this great desire is the password.

This 'permission' seems to have to be sought at the lowest level of the energy sphere where etheric/energy particles are drawn to the total soul. So if there is a refusal, perhaps the total soul can shed our type of etheric particles, and try to enter another universe. I don't know, it's a surmise. In a way it seems unlikely for it means regression, however slight, and that does not accord with any of the known laws. Somehow I feel that a total soul will be attracted to a universe that will be suitable in the first place. Whatever, one passes in at the gate and is noted by the gatekeeper. That, of course, is a symbolic way of putting it. For the Christ Spirit is the universe and if you find yourself in it, it is because you have been accepted by the Logos of that universe. I doubt that the total soul even notices the acceptance, let alone actually asks. It is, as I said, the desire that matters and is read.

And if the Christ Spirit 'is' the universe, does It reside in any particular part of Its Universe? Do we not say to one another 'God is everywhere'? This Christ Spirit is the God we took to be the one who created us, It is the one we thought omnipotent. Everything you ever thought of 'God', or the other names it has been called through the ages, is this Spirit, this Logos. Now can you see how much more is the Great Spirit?

It is how we approach this new way of looking at a being that we have always thought of as GOD that is now of paramount importance to us and the future generations of souls in your earth world. This is the crux of this whole book. We must not make the mistakes of the past. We will make too many of our own to repeat others.

Fear must not be inculcated. Dread must be a thing of the past. Blind worship must be turned to knowledgeable admiration and respect. Interaction between the souls and their God must be as free as their will, untrammelled by any who say their ability 'to know God' is better than the ordinary person, and only they can talk to God for them.

There will be those who show the way and may give explanations to help those who have difficulty in understanding. There will be those who will comfort the bereaved, lonely and homeless, who will heal and nurse the sick, sit with the dying. There will be those whose knowledge is obviously greater but they must be the most humble. If their knowledge is truth they cannot but be humble, for they know the karma, the effect, that will come upon them if they do not teach the truth in all humility. But do not mistake ability and confidence for lack of humility. To stand before even one person and teach takes great courage and faith that they speak the truth.

Yet there will still be differences in what these teachers say. Look therefore for the similarities and when they cross and re-cross you can be sure there is a pearl lying within the teaching. Still test with your reason all that is said or written, particularly my very own words on these pages. Accept only as your own conscience dictates, for although it may not be correct, it will be right for you.

Chapter 10

Down to Earth

And so we come back down to earth, from our rarefied mental wanderings among new ideas and propositions, back to a world of burgeoning terror, megalomania, and material greed. Who, does it seem, would give up a moment of their time to consider the fact that once, aeons ago, they were an Angelic being, that they might become one once more in the far flung future? Who cares that animals, let alone minerals and vegetation, are our immediate past, that the present animals are the humans of the future? Who cares about anything except themselves and what they can acquire for themselves? The answer is – more people than you would suspect. But they are not the sort of people whose ideas and thoughts gain much credence or popularity in the world.

Nearly all people ask such questions as – why, oh why, does life on this physical planet we call earth appear to include so much pain, unhappiness and torment? Why are there those who do the most terrible things to others? Why the unfairness of it all? The sick, the cripple, the war weary, the poor, the homeless, and yet there are those that have so much they could feed and keep an army of people with their possessions and wealth if they cared to do so. Why are there some who wish to kill all who do not 'think' as they do? Why do some have too many children and 'God' deny even one child to another couple who long for a baby of their own? We could fill a chapter with our whys.

I wonder if my explanations of the Spiritual Universe have given you one iota of light on these perplexing questions? Probably not, for you have not yet really been shown how to apply these explanations, nor been given some that lie nearer your own condition. The condition of being a human on the planet earth in the latter end of the twentieth – beginning of the twenty-first century. This then is what we must do, this second time round the journey of the soul, in the last chapters of this book of mine. In doing this, you will find that it covers what we have only touched upon lightly in passing in discussion about the practical nature of the journey of the soul, that is to say the moral, ethical, and spiritual values and nature of your cosmic life in the Spiritual Universe.

*   *   *   *   *

In the pre-Etheric/Physical Universe the soul has chosen its positive or negative path and followed its course through its various lives with this principle dictating in some respects what it will choose to be. They are all things that do not cause 'premeditated' harm or good. In other words they just are. They are the spirits of the Universes. In every context the two play off against each other. This continues on into the Etheric Universes, down through their descending layers of density to the physical itself. In

fact right up to the moment that the soul turns the corner
and starts to take itself on the long journey home. Until
this moment, it has occasioned no wrong nor yet no
good. For it did not know how to do either. That it
caused difficulty or even harm to another is neither here
nor there, for it was only doing what it was supposed to
do.

This we must consider. Premeditated. That is the key
word. Let us use a symbol.

A virus, say a particularly vicious form of 'flu virus,
infects the man of a family. He becomes sick and has to be
off work. The family is poor and the loss of income makes
matters worse. The virus spreads round the family and all
suffer pain and discomfort. Then even worse disaster
strikes. The beloved grandfather is infected and it is too
much for him and he dies, a great loss to the rest of the
family.

Now you may say that virus was bad, even evil in the
devastation it caused to that family. You might hate it; you
will certainly do all you can to kill it. Yet all it has been
doing is living in its own environment, your body, using it
to have its own being, just as you use all that is about you.
It has caused harm, devastation to its environment, but
then, so do you! Are you evil? I bet you don't regard
yourself as that. You would say you only take what you
need to live. So does the virus. It does not enter your body
saying to itself 'I hate you. I am going to cause you the
most harm and pain I possibly can'.

But perhaps another human being comes along who
happens to have a pathological hatred of the man of this
family and wishes to do him harm. If then, they had access
to a phial of the deadly virus, took it and threw the
contents of it into the face of the man, causing all the

above to happen, this would constitute a completely different outlook on the subject.

In the first instance, the virus had no hatred to work out. No harm was intended or known to be done. In the second instance, there was evil intent, premeditated thought to cause harm. But that was only on the part of the human. The virus itself was still just as innocent. It could not possibly know how it was being used. It still went about the business of gaining its living, keeping its existence going.

This then is the great difference in pre-human souls and those who have discovered that certain something, that realisation of individuality, that there is a them and me, that what they do affects others and the doing must be tempered with the thought of the good or harm it may do. This then is the beginning of personal responsibility.

It is also the beginning of what the Eastern people of your world have named 'KARMA'. This is a pearl buried in religions that is most important. Westerners know it as repeated in Christian teachings often paraphrased as 'As ye sow, so shall ye reap'. Yet it is not thought of in quite the same way as Karma. We ourselves said it was the old way of saying the law of cause and effect. Even this law is not quite what Easterners think of as Karma.

The Christian statement is taken to mean that a punishment or a withholding of reward is the reaping, most probably in the 'Next World', after earthly death. Good actions will be rewarded in like manner. Occasionally dreadful things befall the evil doer and seem like a retribution, but mostly we remark that 'The ungodly flourish like a green bay-tree'. In other words, they seem to get away with their wickedness.

Now Karma, on the other hand, can happen at any

time, during the life that the deed was committed or during the next life, or even several lives on. It is also concerned with other actions beyond the context of whether they were good or evil, like service to the things of the Spirit, service to the unfolding of knowledge and wisdom within oneself. Our interactions with our fellows, our loves, our hates. Repayment of debts to our fellows, not only putting right a wrong action but seeking and accepting their forgiveness and making restitution. On the other hand, there could be a debt of gratitude that must be repaid, a lifetime of love and devotion to be returned. Or, looking at it from the other side, you may be the one to whom the devotion must be returned, or after an ill deed, restitution made, forgiveness sought. You must give the opportunity for this to happen, for it was also something pertaining to your life as well as to the perpetrator.

Something that must be worked out – that is the key to Karma. It is not so much a retribution as is posed in the idea of the sowing and reaping of one's deeds. I must tell you that I think the original teaching had more of the Eastern idea of Karma in the giving of this symbol than what Christians later made of it. This is no more than what was done with the idea of Karma itself.

It was thought that Karma pertained to almost anything: lower forms of life, countries, nations, the whole world. I personally do not think this is so because these things are all formed of the pre-human soul that did not, could not, conceive good or harm but just existed. This is my own feeling and that of most of my teachers, but there are yet others who disagree. Of course, the law of cause and effect operates throughout the total Spiritual Universe and when the soul takes or makes an action there will be a result. But it is not thought to accrue any personal

Karma to that particular soul. This action of the law is a different idea entirely from the personal accumulation of a Karma, responsibility for the acts. I concede that it is just possible that the highest manifestation of animals that are cohabiting with human type souls and just about to turn the corner into individualisation may be creating their first Karma in the fact that they owe the human for 'bringing out their soul!' Yet it has often been repaid already in that life-time by unstinting devotion and companionship.

At first the Karma would be mild, for the soul would not have learnt yet the meaning of good and harm. This, as I have said before, is the important point. It is the thought behind the deed that is more important than the deed itself and, yet even one step more removed, the whole philosophy behind the thought, behind the deed, the building of the total character.

What then is this Karma? Has it a substance? Can one see it, measure it, so that it may be paid back in equal quantity, good or bad? Yes and No. On your world it is not possible to see it, only to experience its effects. But you will recall that I have told you in the etheric realms thoughts actualise and the state and progression of a soul can be seen. This state and progression is dictated by the soul's Karma. For Karma is like a record of the soul's attempt to learn and grow. It is done by the operation of the law of cause and effect, as so much is in the Spiritual Universe. It is not only a record but the most perfect justice. It is not so much a punishment, but there for the soul's health and growth. It may mean that a soul suffers a particularly harrowing set of circumstances but it will be exact in its measurement of what that soul caused to happen to others and, and this is most important, extracts only what it needs to make it see and understand why what it did was harmful.

You will note I talk about 'harm' rather than 'wrong', yet still talk of good. This is because there is so much muddled thinking about wrong, wrongdoing, evil and most of all 'sin'. This thinking in itself has caused harm, for it does not make the perpetrator realise the thoughts behind the deed, nor yet make them change their general attitude.

Sin is punished. Wrongdoing is punished. A man steals, goes to prison and when released is said to have paid his debt to society. What a nonsense! The debt is to the person he stole from in the first place and no-one else. Shutting him up in a cell with others of like mind teaches him absolutely nothing, even if conditions are harsh and he is made to do hard labour. It does not relate to the wrong he actually did. He does not see what harm he did. At last this is being better understood in modern society but there is still a long way to go.

What is difficult to understand, then, is about the effects of Karma that happen in a next, or even one after that, life. How does the soul know, when locked up in an uncomprehending physical body, that this rigour or joy is happening because of something else that happened, something that it cannot even remember from a previous life? This is because you do not appreciate the continuous thread of existence – especially Westerners but some Easterners also. When you step out of the physical and return to the etheric the total results are there to be seen. The record is there to be seen in the Akashic Records and it can be computed what has to be done to eliminate the faults, help the soul to learn and decide what will repay the debt. Some will not even be bothered, hardly be aware of this record and care even less. They will plunge back into physical life and not understand that their Karma will happen whether they know about it or not. It will still be just, whether they learn from it or no. Somewhere, sometime, they will scream out *'Why is this happening to me? Somebody please help me!'*. It could be in a physical life or it could be while in an etheric interval. That heartfelt cry always brings help.

The help comes from the guardians and guides of that particular soul who will patiently explain or lead the soul to an explanation. If the soul gains the wisdom, it will then choose lives that lead towards a greater harmony. It will seek to repay debts, suffer hardships to gain understanding of them and try to change the thinking behind everything it does. All in that place of the closed book where one sees if one has remembered the lesson, the schoolroom of life. Lastly, in later stages the soul will actually recognise a dose of Karma when it happens and that will be because it has started to feel the effects of the love-power at its centre as it makes its way to the surface. It activates the senses of the soul.

So Karma is almost a tool used to develop the awakening spirit of the soul after the long, long sojourn in the innocent forms of pre-individualisation. That is what I will mean by the word Karma. It is, after all, another one of those things which has had much appended to it, in common with other religious ideas of your world.

We have talked about 'working it out' and this is done by our continuing interactions with those about us. There are so many ways this 'working out' can occur that it would be impossible to enumerate them. Generally, a set of circumstances happen in one life (or it can be in the intervening etherical realms) whereby one soul causes, or actually does something to another soul. A hurt or a healing, they have loved or hated, helped or hindered, accepted or rejected, cared for or cast off, the list is endless. Then depending on the thought behind the perpetration of the deed, the knowledge of the result before the action was taken or conversely, the lack of care, consideration and selfishness in any action, there will follow, somewhere, sometime, a returned action of a nature that will either compensate or create the circumstances to bring the soul to realise its own mistakes. The justice of these returned actions has to be seen to be believed. How often you hear people say 'It was poetic justice' when retribution falls on one who has caused a similar discomfort to another. Karma is more than poetic justice, it is perfect justice, for it is of the Great Spirit in which all is perfect.

Here we come to a difficult question. Does 'God' cause us problems, does the Great Spirit tempt us to sin and does It allow us to suffer, even cause it to happen? It does seem as if I have said that in the last paragraph, about the justice of the Great Spirit. It is not that It exactly causes anything to happen to us, but we have our being within Its Spiritual Universe and we are subject to the laws, laws that, as I have said before, are not fiats, promulgations, or decrees. They are natural laws that make the Universe exist. You cannot change the law of gravity. You may find ways of suspending it, reversing it by using your wits, but you cannot change it.

Nor can you change the law of Karma, cause and effect. You may avert it, get round it, suspend it – for a while – but it is still there. What you have to get rid of is the idea that somewhere there is a being actually looking at every tiny happening and apportioning out an equal return happening. There is a continuing power, force, call it what you will, that just works automatically. It is certain that it is connected with the Akashic Records, and that with knowledge these records can be consulted and read, but how, or even if they do more than record, is not known. There does not seem to be a keeper, or writer of these records although there are great souls who will assist any who seek help to transcribe and understand the records.

Exactly where they are is a difficult question too. The answer seems to be, like the Great Spirit, everywhere, possibly written on one's very own Spark of Divinity, for that after all is part of the Great Spirit. Or it is through that Spark that one passes to a dimension where this record is, exists. Today, for the first time in history, you are a generation that can understand the principles of recording something, something so real as to almost be the actual thing. You move towards holographic, almost moving, living, breathing representations of happenings. This is how the Akashic Records appear to one when consulted. Whether this is their true form I don't know, but it is certainly suitable to our needs. I do know that one has to go into a kind of subliminal experience to see these pictures, these records, yes, even we of the higher earthly etheric realms.

Many of you in physical form have seen them too and write and record these happenings. You have not always realised that was what it was and tell each other tales of 'lives flashing before one as one was dying' or being shown pictures of one's life when you had appeared to die. The dying did not occur at that time and the memory could be recalled and told to others.

I think that 'Karma' goes a long way to explain the many different conditions of mankind found on earth. The happenings that seem to befall one, good or bad. 'Lucky old so and so, everything he touches turns to gold', we say, and 'Poor old so and so, nothing ever seems to go right for him'. Perhaps the lucky Midas gave all he had in his last life and is given a chance to have worldly possessions in his new life. Perhaps the second poor soul had all the luck in the world last time round and misused it.

But there could be a different way of looking at it. Midas may *need* the lessons of great wealth, for, as we know, it does not always bring great happiness. Poor old 'Out of luck' may have used up all of his stored luck and did not put anything back in, is bankrupt, for remember, 'As ye sow, so shall ye reap'. If you have not put out, you will not earn anything back in. So where you might be thinking that the rich soul in his life is the more reprehensible of the two, for somehow the rich are always imagined to be less spiritual than the poor, it could be that poor old 'Out of luck' is lower down the scale of progression.

All very complicated, and it teaches one not to judge by outward appearances on your earth. For you may think that a soul locked up in a badly deformed body is being 'punished' by Karma, forced to experience pain, discomfort, and you may ask, 'What terrible thing did he do in his last existence then, that he has to suffer so much now?'. Now, I am not saying this never happens, but it is just as likely that a soul of great magnitude and advancement may be taking that life to help another learn how to cope with caring for such a one. It may be helping to develop qualities of the soul in another. What a sacrifice!

One last thing. It could be that the return of Karmic

force is not administered by the one against whom an action was perpetrated. But once the wrong of that action was realised, then forgiveness must be sought from the wronged and possibly compensation given to them by the wrongdoer. Sometimes this is done by a face-to-face confrontation in the etheric realms and sometimes it is on the physical plane, and although still face-to-face, the parties do not know that this is what is happening. This accounts for the many oddities and strange happenings in life.

Having looked at one of the things that affects all souls in their human existence, let us now look at the question of souls being positive or negative. What do we mean by this 'positive and negative', you might be asking, and how do I know which one I am? Very difficult to answer, particularly the last question. Certainly up to the moment of self-knowledge, the finding of the 'I exist' principle, I do not think the total soul, the soul-cells or the individual souls have the slightest idea whether they are positive or negative. From then on we make guesses, but perhaps only the Great Spirit and the Christ Spirit really know. All we have are clues.

Now on your world the words 'positive' and 'negative' are mostly thought of as relating to things scientific, positive and negative fields in the making of electrical power, positive and negative poles in magnetic studies. But it has been transferred to traits of character, almost a symbol for ideas like a positive way of thinking or negative thoughts, being negative about something. The former scientific things are very provable; you only need the horseshoe-shaped magnet of your childhood to witness its truth. Everyone uses electrical power without a second thought about positive or negative fields. In other words you take for granted something you cannot see because you can see the result of their interaction. The production of electrical power has something to do with positive and negative fields; it doesn't really matter that you don't understand how it works, for you can still use the results to run your sophisticated machines.

Well, we have all been doing just that for aeons of time, using the powers of positive and negative potential throughout the whole of the Spiritual Universe. You recall I said it was almost the first emotion ever experienced that caused this choice, a kind of resentment that some felt and others did not. Well, that triggered a sort of charging which made them 'poles' of one sort or the other in the energy spheres. What might be called raw energy particles of the Great Spirit then pass between them, and become the power of the Spiritual Universe. Do you remember I called them the energy network of the Spiritual Universe? This power is directed by the mind principle to form that which is needed.

As the total souls descend more deeply into this energy existence, they have to follow the ebb and flow of the power. They are subject to it, so to speak, until they learn to control it. The positive souls will find a definite, practical way of doing this and the negative often do it by not fighting it, letting it take them where it will. This is what hastens their 'fall' into matter, often making them miss some of the lessons learnt by the ones using more positive methods and taking a little longer to traverse the sphere. You see the negative are also in a hurry to get back to the Great Spirit, for that is what they resented in the first place, being separated from It.

Now we have two kinds of soul quite clearly developing, haven't we? The one taking its time and gaining knowledge, experience and a certain way of thinking and doing things, and the other which tends to rush through or even bypass these experiences that seem of no importance to it. That these souls are young, new souls or more ancient souls does not seem to matter. Oh yes, just because a soul is ancient it does not mean to say it will be a positive soul. However, the more ancient negative souls do seem to take some time to learn and probably hasten more slowly towards the densest of matter.

Am I beginning to build up a picture? Now I have told you that our universe, the Etheric/Physical, tends to attract more negative souls than positive. In other words we get an imbalance. There are possibly other universes where the balance is the other way. Lucky universes, but ours is not one of them. We are a very gross universe in both our kind of etheric material and particularly in its lower form, the physical. It forms into things very easily, possessable things. While this is very useful in learning the physics of the Great Spirit, it can also lend itself to less high minded things than gaining knowledge. It lends itself to the reprehensible desires of greed, gain and acquisition.

Engineers love the Etheric/Physical Universe for its hard practicality in holding things firmly in shape which they can then design and refine. Artists love it for the lasting forms they can create and leave to posterity. Farmers love the solid minerals with which they can form a bond. These are some of the positive uses of the Etheric/Physical Universe. Yes, although our etheric is more tenuous than the physical it nevertheless is really quite firm in its holding possibilities, more so than other universes.

This firmness then attracts those who do not find the

acquisitions of the mind as alluring as something which they can see and possess. This includes a body! A body that can enjoy the acquisitions, experience carnal pleasures and gain power over others. In gaining the body one might say, they lose their soul.

Well, we know that is not true, don't we? What they lose is 'sight' of their soul. It takes a soul of quite some ability and stature to retain sight of their inner spark of divinity, that part which is the Great Spirit. At least retain a sense, a feeling of its presence, and not cover it entirely in gross matter.

By now you must be realising that a world sinking into materialism must be drowning in its preponderance of incarnating negative souls, each one trying to get its share of the booty, the goods and chattels, the 'things' it can acquire in a world where more and more things are available to be owned. But also more and more souls are trying to be the owners of those things. It is easy to see what will happen in those circumstances. Some will go to the wall, be defeated, trodden underfoot.

There are representatives of the positive incarnating, obviously, for there is still the need for the two fields so that the particles may flow between them and therefore create, be, exist. This has gone on happening to what might be called raw energy and substance right down the line of all the spheres and is even happening to you right now as you sit reading this book. Indeed it is the power that holds your book together!

But here, for all I have said about vicious negatives incarnating on your world, I must dissuade you from an idea that is very prevalent. That is -

Positive equals good – Negative equals bad.

This is NOT true.

This will need a lot of explanation, so let us therefore leave it for the next chapter. I leave you with a consoling thought. The fuel that the souls of Earth produce is particularly fine and superior in nature. When it is eventually found and transported homeward there is great rejoicing, for it is of a very valuable nature to the Spiritual Universe. Now I do not know this for myself but I have been assured this is so by the highest of sources with which it has been my good fortune and blessing to have had contact.

Chapter 11

Heart of the Matter

What does all this information mean to me? How am I supposed to make use of it and if so in what way may I use it? Of what relevance is it to my life? These are the kind of questions that I feel you should or will be asking by this point in the book. I would like to talk about this before I plunge into further information.

All that has gone before in this book will be, to you, a supposition. If these suppositions are true or seem at least sensible, logical enough to you to be true, if you feel there is a likelihood of truth, then you cannot help but ask the above questions or something like them.

Am I now, in these last chapters, going to give you a format for living your life, ways to follow, precepts to keep, and tell you what is right and wrong, what you may do or not do, what is moral or immoral, perhaps give you new 'Holy Laws' to follow? — *NO, I AM NOT!*

That is not what this book is about. That is to say, it is not a book that sets out to teach a way of living. It is a book that only intends to give you all the facts, the actualities of the Spiritual Universe that you live in, how it works and how you come to exist within it and journey around it. With that information I expect you to be able to work out how your life should be conducted and why. Do I disappoint you? I'm sorry. But have I not said, it is considered that mankind has now improved his intelligence, his capability to understand, his ability to perceive. It is a book written with his increased intelligence taken into consideration. It is a guide to the Spiritual Universe and not intended as guidance on how to live your life.

We hope, however, with these facts given to you, you can see why your life should be lived in a particular way and adjust your precepts accordingly, not because you are told to do so but because you can see good reason for doing so. You are beyond being 'told' how to live. You are on the threshold of an age where you should 'know' how to live, know how and 'why'. Self responsibility. That includes the responsibility to gain the knowledge of how and why you should live in harmony with your fellow souls of all kinds. For in harmony you will find the right way to live.

I do not doubt that this is a philosophy that is more difficult to follow than a set of precepts laid down by another, for it will cause you to actually have to think about it for yourself and take blame for incorrect actions. I am sure leaving it all up to somebody else is an easier course of action, but look around, your world has run on the precepts of one person or another since time was. The people blindly following, obeying Holy Law, putting their wrong-doing on to others without even understanding properly what they had done wrong saying, what does it matter? I can have another go and be 'good' next time round. Does it seem to work? Obeying without understanding the reasons. Whitewashing oneself with the 'blood' of another. Did any of you do any better the next time round and where did obeying all those 'laws' get you?

The people of your world lie in a deep morass of ancient dogmas, unable, unwilling to get up and change themselves, too lazy to even care. Their world, they are constantly told, is becoming a foul place to live because of their even fouler practices. They continue to hate and kill, bomb and maim, put down and enslave their fellow humans. They allow millions to starve to death or go homeless and unclothed. Greed has reached such proportions that you go in constant fear lest another take your possessions. Cruelty to all species, including your own, goes almost unheeded.

The misuse of your world has reached a point where it is not sure it will survive. It appears to be dying. All this is the result of individuals not understanding their nature and the nature of their planet, their universe and the Spiritual Universe in which they have their existence. You are at the point of individualisation and it has to be that every one of you, individually, understands this nature and acts accordingly.

A tall order, you might think. And you would be right. But we must start somewhere, and I have started with this small attempt to help you begin to understand. So I will try only to point out the results of actions and by that you can judge for yourself whether you take these actions yourself or not. You can begin to form your own precepts, each and every one of you. I really don't think you can do any worse than what has gone before.

What I say to you, if I may be allowed just one piece of advice, is:

'Use your intelligence so hardly won by past incarnations of homo sapiens. Study, read, research, investigate, weigh up and decide for yourself in the light of the knowledge gained if an action is right or wrong. Then be willing to accept responsibility for that action.'

It is not that you will always make the correct decision but you are more likely to if you have good information. It is not that you should decide that any particular thing is now what you 'believe' to be true, but rather that at this time, with your present knowledge, it is what you think might, could be true. You should stay open and receptive to further knowledge at all times. Be willing to change, open minded enough to see all possibilities.

We are taught to have three mental pigeon holes. The first is for ideas that are new or are being considered. The second is for those ideas which have been found acceptable and form the main body of opinion at any one time. The third is those ideas not considered to be correct. Note that no ideas are ever totally discarded. Each and every one may be moved to a different pigeon hole at any time if an opinion is changed in the light of new information or knowledge. Unfortunately we do not always come by our knowledge in the correct consecutive order to be assimilated. So if that which was considered incorrect is found to have something to recommend it after all, it can be retrieved and placed in the consideration pigeon hole. If later still it is found to be of value, thought likely to be true, it can again be moved to the acceptable pigeon hole. Likewise, what was thought to be true can later be re-consigned to the incorrect pile if it has not stood the test of time and newly gained knowledge.

This pigeon-holing can go on for ever and has merit in that it helps to keep an open mind, encourages the search for new knowledge and makes a soul grow by its own efforts. Why not try it out for yourself?

With only these recommendations I would like to push on in my practical way and tell you a few more facts before I end my book. What a pile you will have to wade through in your 'being considered' pigeon hole.

*   *   *   *   *

I ended the last chapter with a rather positive statement. In the light of my earlier words in this book it will seem strange, a paradox, that I say positive does not equal good and negative bad. We have looked at the scientific meaning of positive and negative, the actualities of it throughout the Spiritual Universe. Now we must look at it as applied to the soul's character.

What have we said so far? The original choice was because of a kind of resentment. A hardening of a deeply felt loss. Was that loss a wrong thing to feel? Did the total soul do wrong in feeling it? I hardly think so; it was a natural thing to feel and I suspect all souls feel it. What made the soul different was the change of the feeling from sadness of loss to resentment, the very first show of loss of understanding. It could be that the souls go out from the source with the propensity within them before they even leave to become negative. It is sure that both are needed in what might be called the physics of the Spiritual Universe.

If this is so it means, one, that the so-called positive are merely unchanged particles of the source, two, the negative have a built-in difference and, three, there is no choice but just a reality. Two kinds of particles are put forth from the source which appear to be the same at the moment of parting.

Now which is correct, the choice or the *fait accompli?* We don't know. There are many other explanations offered, I assure you, and they are debated endlessly by those interested in such things. I am but showing you that I too still consider all possibilities, have my mental pigeonholes. One thing is certain, something causes there to be positive and negative souls.

I said that drifting down through the spheres various things happen to the formation of character of souls because of these polarities. They choose certain kinds of experiences, things to be. The negative veer towards the unhelpful, and the positive the other way. If the negative are feeling resentment perhaps they are seeking ways to get revenge, to hurt, to hit back, blindly and not even at what they thought caused their unhappiness. For is that not what resentment is, a feeling of loss of esteem, of love? Returned by saying, 'I won't love you either'. That the loss of love is not true is neither here nor there.

Could it be that it is just one more tool in the Spiritual Universe to cause us to find the fuel? Drive us, rather as earthly instincts in animals drive them to survive. Imagine if there was only one polarity. All positive or all negative. There would be no movement, stagnation.

The difficulty then is trying to see why a physical fact should affect the nature of a soul, its character, its particular way of coping with the Spiritual Universe it finds itself within, its interactions with others. Now we have said that up until the moment of individualisation the souls were not conscious of causing harm. You will recall my symbolic story of the virus. Nevertheless, that will be precisely what the negative souls will have been doing in greater and greater quantity, the deeper into matter they went. Reacting with more and more resentment to all with whom they come into contact. Losing sight of the source more quickly and with it understanding. Missing important experiences, lessons, and consorting with like souls, picking up untoward knowledge. For the negative learn all the physics of the Spiritual Universe, just as much as the positive.

This leaves us thinking the positive are rather goody-goody types, who don't skip classes, do their homework, keep their noses clean and never make mistakes or do anything harmful. Wrong. It leaves us thinking that all negatives go round causing pain and harm, are bad pupils and never do an action of good. Wrong again.

The truth is somewhere in between. Let us look at your earthly meaning of positive or negative traits of character.

Positive: Strong-willed, tenacious, looks to the good things happening rather than bad, believes they will happen.

Negative: Lacks will, gives up easily, thinks that the worst will always happen rather than the good, believes the worst will happen.

This is obviously not what we have been talking about. There is nothing 'evil' in the negative traits; a positive strong will could be used to cruelly dominate another soul. The whole thing is a matter of words. It would really be better to use another term to describe the two types of souls. But what do we use? Yin and Yang? They too have nuances of meaning in their own language which do not work in this instance. Right and Left? Of what? Good and Bad? What is good to one is bad to another. Right and Wrong? The same applies.

For, in truth, positives do not always do good and negatives do not constantly do wrong. Positives do not always show strength and if they do, they do not always use it in the right way, for good purposes. Negatives are not always the grabbing greedy, nor the tyrant. Often they can be the downtrodden. It is answered in the fact that each soul is not totally positive or totally negative. They are not wholly or fully charged one way or the other – but – some are; they are particularly positive, particularly negative. Souls do 'tend' more to one way than the other. It does appear that the more negative a soul is, the more propensity it has to express hate, which leads to evil deeds. The very positive soul seems to be more able to express love which therefore leads to deeds which do good. For hate is the negative of love. It is the same emotion reversed. If a heart is full of hate it does not perform deeds which do the hated any good. Conversely, a heart full of love will do nothing to harm the beloved.

And so we have all stages in souls of positive and negative with a balance set half-way within themselves. The scales will tip over the half towards one pole or the other which makes them express more of that pole than the other, but they are capable of expressing both. The more over the half-way point they are, the more of that pole they express. It leads one to ask if there are any that are totally positive or negative, incapable of expressing the other. Are there any such in our own universe of the Etheric/Physical? Indeed there appears to be, but whether they are even then, totally, one or the other, incapable of expressing the opposite pole, I don't know. Who would be an almost totally positive soul is easy if you think about it.

It is the Christ Spirit, that Spirit which is the creator of this universe in that Its being was the first cause, the positive pole that matter passed. If that is so it is logical to expect that it passed between It and a negative pole. A very strong negative pole. A pole that in its way was just as necessary as the positive pole. Is this pole an actual spirit, a soul? If so, who or what is it?

It is an ancient soul, a total soul that is almost as incomprehensible to us as the Christ Spirit. It has been expressed on your earth as the Devil, or given the form of many demons and devils, depending on what part of the world the idea came from. Unfortunately this gives the picture of satyrs – hoofed, horned, tailed beings of fantasy. It is no more this than God is an old man in the sky, half hidden in clouds.

This might make you feel we have strayed into fantasy ourselves. I assure you we have not. It is the basic fact of the creation of our universe. It is what caused, as you term it, the big bang.

Ah, do I see light dawning? You must be following logically on from my previous information. I said the passing of energy and matter between the poles of the souls of the Great Spirit created, formed the different spheres, each according to that sphere. The Logos was sent out to form a new universe within the Spiritual Universe of the Great Spirit. It is logical to suppose that an equally negative force must have been sent out as well, something that would cause the greatest of charges to pass between two poles, enough to cause there to be formed enough substance to make an entire universe, and continue to hold it together.

Where you go wrong, man and womankind, if I may be so bold as to point it out, is that you imagine these spirits to be in your own likeness, your own earthly, bodily likeness. They are not.

The only likeness is the particle at their centre, the particle that is the Great Spirit. In this they are the same. That they exist by the same laws of the Great Spirit as yourself is so. The rest is something you – and I – cannot begin to even imagine. This is why we call it 'Spirit'.

The Great Spirit – The Unfathomable Ultimate. The Christ Spirit – Ineffable. The Diablo Spirit – Indescribable. We can only see, experience their effect.

What took place and still takes place between the positive and negative Spirits of our universe is thought of in your world, symbolically, as a battle. Hence the 'Final battle of Armageddon' between the forces of 'Good and Evil'. It is not really a battle but merely the power of the Great Spirit in which 'ALL' have their being, working things out, creating the possibilities of finding that which is sought, the fuel of the Spiritual Universe. Each plays its part, large or small. Each creates circumstances in which the fuel can be garnered, in smaller or greater quantities. What we have to come to terms with is that what we call 'Good and Evil' both reside within the Great Spirit.

Look again at what I expect you have read without daring to really take in, what it means in my chapter entitled, *'The Great Spirit and The Logos'*. I postulated that the Christ Spirit is what mankind thought of as 'God', everything that is good. This is what the Christ Spirit is: the most positive soul in this Etheric/Physical Universe. The one that can express love more fully than any other here in this universe. But I have said that this is not the final, the ultimate as was previously thought. It is what the Great Spirit has set out for us while we have lost sight of Its own being.

How wise is the Great Spirit, for how difficult it is for us to understand that both good and evil are within It, are It. The two of everything, Yin and Yang, positive and negative, good and bad, hate and love, and so on for ever and ever. If you hold a stick in the centre it has a definite termination at one end and another at the opposite end. Two definite points. Yet the stick is undoubtedly one. A symbol. A picture idea to try to make you understand what is incomprehensible.

We have not been entirely wrong in thinking that the Christ Spirit was God, was the Great Spirit, for in truth It is a wonderful personification of that Spirit. But then so are we personifications of that same source, regretfully not so wonderful.

Somehow we can understand that one spirit personifies good and another bad. That is at our level of understanding. That these spirits interact with one another is understandable. That we have made them out to be little more than superior mankind is understandable, But it is now an idea with which we must begin to dispense. For these spirits do not exactly personify here on your earth, nor any other part of our universe, themselves. They do direct lesser spirits, what might be termed 'their forces', to take form in our universe. This includes every soul from when it enters the gateway of the universe to when it exits. What happens between the two is our whole existence in the Etheric/Physical Universe.

These universal powers act upon our own souls depending on the balance of positive and negative we have within us. It is this balance, not being wholly one or the other, that makes it so difficult to decide which we are, positive or negative. It is this balance that makes us – all of us – capable of doing good or evil. It is this balance in us that makes us able to love or hate. For we are the Great Spirit and if both are within It, then both are within us. I suspect that even in the most positive spirit, or the most negative, there lies just a tiny amount of the opposite. If not, they would not be of the Great Spirit, which is impossible.

Why did I say that all souls became positive or negative in the total soul stage and not 'partly' one or the other, a mixture of both? Please forgive me, for it has been the way in which I have led you to consider new ideas, a stratagem which I have used. I give you a fact which I appear to alter later in the book. It is not so much an alteration as a modification. For instance, take what we have just been discussing. If I had said right at the beginning of this book that the souls became partly positive and partly negative, it would have been extremely tedious to explain at that point. Now you have been so good as to follow me thus far, and I have been able to tell you about so many things, it is easier for me to enlarge on a subject. So to say the total souls were positive or negative was an easily assimilated fact. I could continue with the rest of my narrative. But you are intelligent. You can see that there are not all positive or wholly negative people around and about you. They are displaying something of both traits. So now I can reveal that your intelligence is working well. You can see that it is a mixture of both polarities in each with a preponderance one way or the other. That preponderance is what I meant in the first place.

It also, if you will allow your intelligence to take you a little further, has shown you the make-up of the Great Spirit of the Spiritual Universe. For if you can see that there are both poles personifying at your level as good and evil in those around you, in your own self, your own soul, and if your soul is the Great Spirit or a particle of the Great Spirit, then surely it is possible to concede that 'Good and Evil' reside with the Great Spirit, and both are of the Great Spirit.

Now we must face the most difficult task of all. That is to understand how, if all are the Great Spirit, the negative, particularly the strongest negatives, can ever learn not to resent and relearn or remember how to love. For we have said that is the key to progress, the fuel, and remerging with the Great Spirit, something for which the negative soul particularly longs. The answer may lie in the heart of the Great Spirit Itself.

For it is as if the Great Spirit is the greatest of all positive poles and Its Spiritual Universe is the negative. I said *'As if'*. Of course we only have theories. Perhaps the balance is even within this ultimate form of existence. Perhaps even here there is mostly positive with a little negative and therefore the central heart expresses mostly goodness and love. The body, Its universe, is the opposite where goodness and love are harder to find and where evil and hate are expressed more fully. For both heart and body, the central power source and the Spiritual Universe, *are The Great Spirit*. This seems to be the answer whichever way you turn. Both poles are needed by the Great Spirit.

As the soul loses its 'expression' of the negative, loses its resentment, it is then as loving as the positive, for both were love as they went out on the journey. The positive will equally have 'expressions' it will have to lose before remerging. This refining, this loss of the expressions of unlove, is learnt on the homeward journey

So it was necessary for the continuance of the Spiritual Universe that the negative did express themselves while out on the journey, made the body more negative. But as they return home, and why should they not do so, they have done their work; they again lose this expression of negativity until they finally join with the source. It is this that makes those that theorise about such things think that even the source conforms to the pattern, the same laws, and has a little of the negative within it.

This then is the position. In the formation of human character we have two major considerations, the amount of positive or negative force in any soul and the Karma that soul has built up since its moment of individualisation. One has been a contributory factor almost, and even maybe from the moment it left the Great Spirit, the other being added later. Of course one could say that the sum total of the soul's experience is another factor and that is true. We are all sum totals of our experience. It colours our choice for the future. There is one other factor we have not looked at yet. That is the age of the soul, whether it is anything from a brash new soul to one of the ancients.

What do we really mean by this? I have talked about the total souls having smaller numbers of soul-cells and those soul-cells having smaller numbers of souls within their make-up. I have also said that this is possibly because the constituent members were in themselves merged souls, that on previous journeys they had been of larger numbers. This is what is thought to be the answer, for it is hard to find an alternative explanation.

Consider. The returning soul merges with the source, becomes that source. We do not know if within that source the soul loses complete identity or not, if, when the time comes for a particle to be asked to go forth, it is precisely the same particle, or whether it has been, so to speak, rearranged with other particles. For when the ones we call the Ancients come forth they do not exactly have memories of other journeys. What they have is abilities that seem to be naturally within them, abilities that are quickly awakened as soon as the experiences of existence start happening. They also seem to have a natural aura of power about them, a knowing quality. The smaller the numbers in the soul, the greater is this power, this quality. They do not know themselves, if asked, if the answer to their smaller numbers is the condensing of the souls to form one, but they themselves have put this theory forward as a possible answer.

This lack of actual memories is a little like your own loss of memory while in the flesh of human form. You can recall your memories, should you wish to do so, every time you finish one of your short lives. I have said these souls use their knowledge in helping to build universes, to give advice. I must now qualify that in that it is this inner power, a kind of instinct, that they draw upon, but remember, the older, smaller soul has one other factor. It can reach back to the source and draw from there directly. The greater the soul the more it can do this. Why then does it not answer the riddle of why it does not remember details of other journeys? They have asked, I am quite sure.

The only answer, so I have been told, is that, if it was not so they would not have the wonder of discovery to push them on. They would have nothing for which to search. Perhaps this is another answer to our own riddle of why we don't recall other lives while in a physical body. It makes each life a journey of wonderment and discovery, a new search for knowledge. Yet could it not also answer the riddle of why some have talents? Talent that is just born within some. The knowledge is already there, has been acquired somewhere before and in the new life it only needs that deep memory, deeper than the physical brain, a memory written on the spirit mind or even as deep as the soul, to have the ability burst forth anew in the new body.

So it is with the Ancients. This greater ability to learn,

to assimilate knowledge and natural talent to manipulate the elements of the existences they pass through gives the older souls more scope. It also brings more responsibilities.

What diversity we can ring from these considerations, every kind and condition of soul that can be imagined and a million more. The permutations are endless. Every one on the peregrination of the soul, wending and weaving its way through the Spiritual Universe, either being a part of the fabric or personifying as something or someone, each causing effects and effecting causes. Each bring their particular character to bear upon a situation, whether it is more negative or positive, if, once individual, it has some Karma to work out, whether it is a soul of ability or learning the skills for the first time – and all the shades in between, all the different levels. Your own society is a microcosm of this diversity. As it is on your world it is throughout the Spiritual Universe; there are all different levels of souls at any one time.

In you, the individual reading my words, there is then a cross-section of all these considerations that make you the kind of soul you are. You may tell me that your bodily conditioning and environment had a lot to do with that too. True in a way, but you either chose, or had those conditions chosen for you because of your previous Karma, be they anything from great wealth and power to abject poverty and unbearable bodily ill-health. It is then how you cope with, deal with, use and learn from those conditions that really matters.

For you are in the heart of physical matter at this time and yours is the struggle. The struggle to understand 'Why?' and 'What is it all for?'. You, my reader, the one for whom these words are written, are the reason for it all.

You, the seeker, are what it is all about. You are the answer to your own question. All that has gone before was to bring you to this point of realisation that there must be a reason for it all. You are individualisation plus. You are the cream of individualisation that has come to the top. From now on you will not so much be a journey of discovery of outward things, experience of things, existences without oneself, but will turn inward and make the greatest discovery of all. Now you will begin to discover the unlimited intricacies of your own soul, the Great Spirit, and both are of the Great Spirit.

Chapter 12

Personal Matters

We cannot all be mystics in this oh so practical world. Those people who are termed 'mystics' try to push back the frontiers of the mind. They seek to define the soul within. Often their ideas are rejected or only accepted by a few. What is difficult is that they are not thought of as doing a job. You cannot all be mystics, you say, wasting time trying to define the indefinable. Yet when you are seeking for yourself you come and ask the full-time mystics to tell you their secrets. You ask them 'Who am I?'. You ask 'What is it all about?' and 'Why?'. You want to understand all this without any effort on your part. You scorn the mystic, reckon he or she is wasting their time, should find a way to earn a living and not expect any help from such as yourself. Well, the mystic, luckily, is usually satisfied with very little but he or she still has to survive. Remember that when you come to consult them.

When the time comes that the questions within any soul have grown to the proportions that they have become a seeker, it is to mystics, or records of mystics, that the soul turns for help, often to find, in the end, that the advice is to become a kind of mystic themselves. Outward knowledge can only take a soul so far. The reading, research, talks and discussions with the knowledgeable always lead to the point when a personal effort has to be made to seek the truth within. That is a joyful moment if the soul accepts the task, for it will only find truth, and each soul is capable of recognising that truth. Between what it finds within and what it has learnt from without itself it is well on the way to beginning to understand its place in the universe and why it is there.

To do this does not mean giving up every waking moment of your time to meditation and study. Not to the ordinary seeker, especially the beginner, the new seeker. Your feet should always be planted firmly on your earth. As time goes by and experience grows, you may find it taking up more of your total life. If it does it is because you have realised its importance.

'But where do I start?' you cry. You have started, by the mere fact that you are reading these words. If you have not already contacted a person or group of people interested in such things, this is something you should do. A book will never replace a live teacher, a sage, a guru. If you just cannot find such people then a book must suffice. I do not intend to lay out any methods of meditation, seeking within, development of the spiritual resources, for there have been many who have come to show you these things and are there now waiting for you to find them. All I will say is test everything that is said or written with your own senses and accept only that which appears reasonable to you. Do not be frightened to disagree. If a teacher is genuine they will rejoice in your questions although they may not always be able to answer them to your satisfaction. Do not denigrate them for this. Each teacher is on his or her own level and is there for others at that level and below. It could be that you have outgrown, outstripped your teacher. Then you must search elsewhere.

But do not think of this as a subject where you can learn all, pass your degree and that will be that. That is precisely the trouble with theological colleges. You can stop your studies at any point but that does not end them. Somewhere in some life you will take them up again and will go on with them until you merge with the Great Spirit where your findings will be used.

In practical terms I suggest you find reputable teachers and organisations that will point you in the right direction. It is up to you to choose or be drawn to the one that will suit your needs. Do not be frightened to attend any gatherings nor to leave them again should they not suit you. Do go with an open, enquiring mind and give them a chance. Sometimes it takes time and several visits to find yourself talking to just the person who can help you. If you are further along the line than this initial stage of seeking, I am most honoured and thank you for having bothered to read my book. I hope it has been of interest to you, and answered a question or two that had not been answered elsewhere. I trust also that it may be of use to you to suggest its reading to seekers who ask your advice. If this happens then I am twice honoured.

But if you are a person who is finding the going a little difficult, then I say persevere. Go at your pace and your level. Do not be intimidated by others who speed ahead, develop abilities, seem to understand quickly. You are you and no one else. If you seek to the best of your ability, you will find that which is right for you. All seekers of every level are the beloved of the spheres, for you, my dear friends, are the garnerers of the fuel. Love and help is poured out, lavished upon you, and you can feel that love and help if you but reach out towards it, just a little.

What exactly would a soul seek within itself should it decide to do so? What is it trying to find? Almost impossible questions to answer, for each soul will find that which is within itself which, of necessity, must be different from any other soul. It is this very difference that is important. It is as if the pieces that compose the Great Spirit puzzle are thrown up in the air to come down every time in a new pattern, find a new form. Each of us is a part in that puzzle and how and where we fall makes up the new pattern. Yes, I know, you recognise symbols now.

There are, however, certain things to be found which are general to all of us, for we all exist under the same laws. The basic 'I exist' principle is the first and foremost, that true concept of realising you 'are'. Here the dimension of time is what helps you understand this principle. Time cannot exactly be seen on your physical world, but it can be measured more surely than elsewhere. More than this, to physically incarnate human souls is the fact of time in conjunction with memory. You are now and you can remember that you were existing seconds, minutes, hours, days and years ago. It is because of that memory of passing time that you can feel your existence in the now. You cannot say for certain that you will exist in the future but the fact that there was a past leads you to expect the possibility of a future. Now outside of the confines of your physical universe, time is of less importance, less impact. You see we – those of us who now reside in the etheric and particularly those who will no longer return to earth – now know that we exist and that there is a future because of our earthly experiences of measurable time.

So time that seems so often to be a tyrant to you, ever marching onward and never waiting for any man, is one more tool used to bring the soul to awareness of itself.

In meditation or study you will find that 'I exist' principle and be able to follow it with the realisation that there are other 'I's, that they too exist. Then extend that to encompass realisations of a larger nature, realise that everything exists. You may say you know that already, but knowing it is not the same as the realisation that you are a part of it all. This then leads to living in greater harmony with your fellow souls of all kinds and conditions. There is so much more one could say but it is not for me to say it. As I have said, there are many teachers of such things. All I will add is that you should take it in stages and eventually it will lead you gradually towards 'Enlightenment', an idea, a word taken from the Buddhist religion.

During this process you will undoubtedly be led by something of which you may not be consciously aware. Depending on your ethnic origin, religion or lack of one, will rest your decision as to what or who this is. For instance, a Catholic might well decide that they feel the presence of a saint. Their religion leads them almost to expect this. A Muslim might expect it to be an Angel or the Prophet. A Hindu might expect it to be the higher self and a Chinese person might expect it to be a relative. A person of no religion at all but well educated might think it is his sub-conscious mind.

Of late, in Western society, there has come into being a 'Religion' called 'Spiritualism'. There are numerous offshoots and similar groups based around this idea. Gradually its ideas have been seeping into society, almost by the back door, for in actual number of Spiritualist churches and societies, they are not exactly in a majority. It has been possible to bring you this book because there was Spiritualism, to bring it through what is termed 'The Veil', from discarnate to incarnate. You will find the basics of this book concur absolutely with Spiritualist thought on the way you live and die. For this is the great truth on which this new 'Religion' was based. It has also propounded many other things found in this book, things like 'self responsibility'.

The most important thing it has done is to make the incarnate aware of the discarnate. It has done this through mediumship. That is, in simple terms, an incarnate person uses a psychic ability to see and hear the forms of those departed, the dead, and relay their messages to other incarnates. They are the medium through which the message passes, the 'one between'. Mostly it is the relations and friends of the incarnate that wish these messages of cheer and love to be passed, but this channel is open to others.

It can, should the incarnate wish, be used by those who have come to teach and guide them. Spiritualists have termed them 'Guides' but I think teachers, helpers, mentors and best of all, friends, are better appellations.

For those who have not got a strong psychic ability of clairvoyance, the inward seeking will often open up another gate to these friends, a mental connection. It is rather like listening to your own thoughts, but there comes a time when it is realised that the thought is new to the seeker. Now learning on an inner plane can start.

Again, in just the same way that knowledge is gathered from outward sources, all ideas and knowledge should be tested by reason and intelligence. *NEVER ACCEPT THAT WHICH OFFENDS YOU.*

This careful scrutiny of inwardly found knowledge should be even more rigorous than before. Never delude yourself, range into fantasy or follow any directions which you consider could be harmful to anyone, wrong or lead to wrongdoing. *NEVER ALLOW DOMINATION BY THIS INNER CONNECTION.*

Because things can get out of hand it is advised that you undertake any meditation or development under guidance of an earthly incarnate instructor. Do not let this put you off a little simple contemplation and study on your own. But when you get further along the road, it is wise to seek help and guidance.

Unfortunately, the seeker will not always find good earthly guidance and that is why I have put in the above strong warning. Those of a known weak psychological disposition should be particularly careful.

What are you trying to accomplish by this study and contemplation? First, you will be satisfying your wish to know, your search for answers. In doing this you will find that it cannot help but influence your view of life, your life. If you have got this far in reading my book and have not found even one tiny point that has affected your views in some way, I would be very surprised. Secondly, it will sort out the views and ideas you do hold. This is where you start using your mental pigeonholes to sort things out. You will be surprised how much you will find already stored there but have not even considered. In meditation these things will come to the top of the pile and you can review them, decide their worth, then replace them in the right pigeonhole. It may be the same one from which it came but then again it might not.

As you progress and learn how to still your own thoughts you will find, now and then, an idea you do not remember having read or been told of before. This will have been given to you from without yourself, by someone who is interested in your development. It will feel like your own idea and this does not matter. The giver will never mind, indeed will be delighted that it has arrived safely. It may be in the form of an idea or it could be almost an experience. The symbol of the Fire in the first chapter was given many years ago in just such a way to the medium writing this book. It changed her views on life and answered many of her 'whys', more so than anything which she had read or heard, for it was found inwardly, a self-realised truth.

It led her towards a better understanding of herself and others. She became more conscious of others and she wanted to do something so that others might be helped to understand themselves. In doing this it might be possible that they too would care more about others and a better world might be the result. This is not exclusive to her. This is what happens to anyone who opens up the doors of the soul. It is the love force being allowed to come through. What is exclusive to her is the form that 'doing' took. Your 'doing' may take any form, any form that is right for you, of which you are capable. It may be world shattering, of huge importance to all mankind, or it may be hidden from general view and seem insignificant to you. It will not be that every soul that is actually in the process of gathering fuel is particularly noticeable to others. For that, my friends, is what you will have started to do. This is what 'the fuel' is all about. For your questing has been the catalyst that will instigate great changes.

Changes to what? To your very soul, that particle of the

Great Spirit within you, the Flame of Life. Change the Great Spirit! Impossible, It is perfect. In Its original source form, yes. But the particles that go forth are a different matter. For remember they have gone forth to find and collect fuel, something that is lacking in them. It takes them aeons of time to find this fuel and during that time the soul has stayed at the heart of them in exactly the same form as it left the Great Spirit. It gave life to everything which they touched, came into contact with, personified as, but unawakened. Now the time has come for the purpose of the journey to begin to be fulfilled. The purpose of the journey is to find ways of expressing love, using love, giving love. It is not enough to just 'feel' love. This is exactly what life in all forms has been trying to teach you and in human-type form particularly. Think hard about that on your own and you will see what I mean. For love is nothing, if not expressed in some way.

From the moment of any soul's enlightenment onwards, it will begin to feel this love force at its centre, and it will seek to express that force in its total existence using the knowledge it has already acquired on so many other subjects. This sets in motion many things, for now the soul is ready to begin to help refuel its Spiritual Universe in which it has its being. It is more than just taking back that which can be made use of by the source, much more. For the soul on the journey upward through the spheres will give back that which it has taken to have all its existences on the downward path. It will be giving back the actual particles it has kept within its make-up from all the spheres, all the levels, all the densities including your own.

As the soul brings the love force through its being in order to express it, the force itself changes, renews and returns the particles to their level, dimension, ready to be re-used by other souls. For there is continuous movement and circulation in everything that exists.

In the same way that the soul could not return to lighter forms but was drawn onwards to denser forms, it is now drawn upwards by the reverse. As it learns to express more love by its 'doings', its work for others, its love of others, rather than self – for it will have learnt to love itself – it loses the densest layer of outer covering. I could say the love force of the soul burns away the layers but this is not quite right. For the actual particles are far from burnt, which to you means destroyed. Rather the force revitalises them for they are worn, used. It is a practical matter of the atoms being rearranged. Your physical body goes back to its constituent parts, at least the body that everyone can see. Yet there has been some release of renewed material even before death if – if the soul has reached the point of its journey where it is bringing through the forces of the soul. For you are much more than the physical shell that you think of as your body.

There are substances that are not observable by the human eye but which are physical. You could not have a physical existence without them. They are the interconnecting particles with the etheric. It is mostly these that are recharged. Have you ever noticed that you often find an ascetic person is generally thin, almost transparent? They eat very little, which is because they do not need a lot of food, for mind is beginning to triumph over matter. They are thin in this way because they are already returning renewed particles to your level. They are one type of soul who are on their last earthly sojourn. Not all take this path.

At the opposite end of the scale, at this time on your earth, there is a great change going on, but it has not yet been effected. Do you recall that I said that as the soul started to incarnate as a human-type it first came as a primitive and later as a tribesman? I mentioned that there were less and less of these tribesmen in which the souls could incarnate. Even the bodies of tribesmen are now of a superior type of homo sapiens and absolutely capable of high intelligence and advanced spirituality. Very few are truly tribesmen any more.

This period, which is now passing, held in its time many forms of the tribesman. It was quite the place to come to have one's incarnations of that level. But the likelihood of finding this kind of life is now disappearing, leaving only a few opportunities for the many souls still wanting to have this type of experience. Although these souls are not ready for the more advanced modern existences, they nevertheless are taking them. They incarnated in bodies of the lowest form of higher homo sapiens. During this last century there has been a fast decline in tribesmen and an equal increase of souls of that type incarnating in higher bodies. The result of this is only too clear on your earth: a massive imbalance of souls with only a rudimentary ability to live in a civilised manner. It is not much good educating them while in the incarnation, for the soul will override the education, ignore it. Education will help a very few, but they will be the ones nearly ready to move forward anyway.

It has meant that every nation has its share of these souls to the despair of the higher minded souls who cannot seem to reach them, try as they might. It causes world population growth without thought, increased crime and violence and seemingly ignorant behaviour. It affects those further along the journey and makes the going difficult for them. The day of the primitive is long over, the day of the tribesman has now passed as well. For you see, it is time for your particular world to be a place where more advanced souls may incarnate, where it is attractive for them to incarnate.

How is this going to be accomplished? It can be attacked in two ways. One is from our side of the veil where many labour to dissuade these lower souls from continuing to incarnate on earth and go to a world which is at the right level for them. The other is for those on your side of life to do everything they can to raise the level of all those who are there; by hard work and a changed way of thinking, make the world and its lower etheric levels unattractive to the lower souls, encourage them to go elsewhere. This has happened elsewhere and it works. None of these lower souls would be anywhere near the time when they had the ability to be gatherers of the fuel.

Conversely you may witness one whom your world terms 'An Old Soul.' This is not quite what is meant by my term, the ancients, the smaller souls of which I have previously spoken. Old souls in this instance means that they have had many earth lives and are reaching their final few or even their last before leaving the earth forever. They themselves may be from an ancient, smaller soul, or a new soul, or any state in between. These souls, nearing the end of their earthly incarnations, are gathering their quota of the fuel instinctively. They may be very simple souls, thought of as morons by all, or they may be highly intelligent souls who hide themselves away and you cannot feel that they are 'doing' anything, not showing love at all.

But you cannot see the pattern that is being woven on

the tapestry of the Great Spirit. You are looking at the back of the material where threads run hither and thither. You can make out blocks of colour here and there that seem to be definite shapes but you cannot be sure. One day you will see the front of the material and know the pattern. It will not be as soon as you die. It will not be when you leave behind the etheric realms of earth. It will not be on the finer worlds of the etheric nor even when you pass back to the Angelic spheres. You will be gradually coming round to the front during this time and the pattern will be becoming clearer the nearer to the front you get. It is presumed that one would finally stand in the position of knowing that vast and intricate pattern somewhere in the sphere of the mind or maybe not even then. It may not be until the actual merging with the source. It takes that long to walk from the back of the material where you now stand to the very front where the pattern can be understood and appreciated.

Do not try to guess what state any other soul has reached, for you will more than likely be wrong about it. Concentrate on your own inner development; that is what is important. Of course you would try to help any who applied to you to the best of your ability, for as you learn, so you too should try to become a teacher. But the greatest teachers of these things never judge the position of any soul, they only love it, whatever its level.

It is the same for those on this side trying to lead and help those who start to search. We do not care what stage they are at; we only feel joy that another soul is on the homeward journey, and those who have made it the thing that they 'do' for others try to bring teaching and encouragement to them.

Yes, that has been the work that I have chosen to do

and also the way I have chosen to work out my own Karma. Ah yes, working it out does not end after the last earthly death, far from it. Some choose to work it out in the etheric rather than the physical. You see, in my last life I tried to concentrate on the things of the soul to the exclusion of all else. I thought it was the most important thing and nothing else mattered. I wanted to bring mankind a better understanding of what I thought was God. I did it in the wrong place, at the wrong time and in the wrong way. I caused harm to be done to many other souls in my charge by my lack of caring. But I did not intend to harm and I searched for that which was right. My motive was good and it won me help and understanding, love from those who watched my struggles. They came to my aid and I was taken and taught the truth of the Spiritual Universe until I understood the enormity of the gap in my knowledge.

I asked to be able to return and bring this knowledge to earth but I was told that it would be thousands of earth years until mankind could even begin to grasp the simplest of its rudiments. I was told it could not be done by one who was incarnate. I knew this was going to be the only way I could work out my own Karma, put right my mistakes. So I had to wait on this side of the veil, making my individual reparations where I could to the souls I had harmed, while always working on the plan which could only be put into operation in a future time. I have been lucky. Some of my soul-cells have come together to help me and we have put ourselves under the direction of far greater souls. We have come to realise that all the time we were a part of the pattern and had been taught and led towards this work.

Now the time is here. Now it is started. The time is

right. Our work is a part of a whole range of plans and operations on both sides of the veil to help the people of planet earth to find their true selves. We herald the age of truth, but it is not yet quite here. There is so much yet to do. We need every seeker and gatherer who has found the knowledge of self to help in this great task. There are many who have come to earth at this time and will come in the next hundred or so years to do this work. Many more range themselves on this side of death, ready to help. We, our group and its work, are just one paving stone put down on the road being built to that new age – one small effort to smooth the way. Our symbolic stone is formed of trying to give an understanding of the Spiritual Universe that mankind might better understand its own corner of that universe.

Chapter 13

Thereafter

If you are near the beginning of your search, maybe all this talk of what you may do to help yourself in your present position, that is to say your present life on the physical earth, is all well and good, helpful, but it probably still does nothing to reassure you about the thereafter. It was hoped that by leading you to study and research, to meditate and consider, you would fill this gap for yourself rather than taking up many pages here in repeating what can be found elsewhere. As I have said, there is any amount of Spiritualist literature on the subject and by diligent seeking you can gain a fair idea of what happens after death. I have explained how it happens and where you go, to the etheric realms that surround this particular planet. There are many books of a Spiritualist nature which give good descriptions of these realms.

The make-up and extent of these realms would take up many of your earth volumes and still would not have explained everything about them. They are vast and so complicated that no one soul will ever see all of them. Some places are so private that none but the maker of those parts will ever see them. Others are made up of the thought forms of many generations being poured into them. For this is the tenor of the etheric realms, their malleability to thought. The completely fixed physical world is left behind. As one journeys away from that fixed state so there is an increase in the etheric's malleability. Those regions close to earth are still of a moderately fixed nature but can be changed if great will is brought to bear on it.

To say that the place is made of a thought form may give you the idea of unreality and impermanence. This is so in the latter case, for when a thought form is no longer needed it does dissipate and disappear. Perhaps this means unreality to you. But what is reality? You perceive objects that appear to be solid to you yet now you know that they are not. They are a constantly moving mass of atoms. You only perceive them as solid. It is the same thing in the etheric realms. When you are there you perceive it as reality and solid. But just as your world could be broken down into its constituent atoms and not gel together any more, so can the etheric. But in the etheric it happens when souls no longer require that particular reality, that particular place. The constituent parts disperse and can be re-used to form something else.

This leads to an unlimited number of realities, places in which a soul can exist. These vary from the densest realms near the physical earth all the way up to the finest, highest realms prior to leaving them forever to exist on the finer etheric worlds. They are the preparation realms for that move. It is in them that you will spend the many years between physical incarnations and after your last earthly life. I have been here over three thousand years. My home is in one of the higher realms, though not the highest, for I have had to stay in a state that would let me return to realms near the earth to do the work of writing this book. But even after all this time there is much that I have not yet seen, experienced.

In the light of our discussions you may be wondering what help it will be to your personal afterlife to become a seeker of the truth within rather than just 'believing' the tenets of a particular faith, accepting their particular idea of the hereafter. The difference is enormous, for the seeker, the meditator, has begun to use their mind, exercise their spirit mind, for you see, the whole of the etheric realms hinges on this ability to use your spirit mind, your ability to create thought forms. It is one of the reasons why art is such an important subject. I don't mean you have to be an artist yourself but it helps. You don't see why? Well rather than tell you, this time I am going to leave it with you as a subject for research and cogitation.

All this is not important right away, at the very second you have death of the physical body, but what does help immediately is that seeking encourages an open mind and so allows other souls to come to your aid, for without knowledge you could easily block them out and not even see them. There's none so blind as those who do not wish to see.

If you have held a distinct idea of what life after death is going to be, you will have created for yourself a narrow view, an enclosed view. It will block out all else until your view changes. That can take a very long time. All the places and ideas of heaven and hell were, in a way, true, because they have been thought to be true and therefore are true. Of course, the prime word there is 'thought'.

As mankind lost sight of the etheric and closed down

its ability to see past the veil it only had memories, and later re-told memories, of what had been seen. It probably wasn't over much in the first place, more the seeing of souls still in the etheric rather than places. Much as a true clairvoyant sees those who are dead today, they appear to be in the clairvoyant's own plane, as if they were still on the earth. With the passing of time the tribes, and later still, whole areas of people, began to make up stories and ideas of what they considered to be an ideal life after death all mixed up with the old racial memories.

A hunter would want a land where the game was easy to catch; a gatherer, a land where it was forever the season of most fruitful abundance, where everything was easy to find; a farmer would want a good and easy harvest. Later in history the town dweller dreamt of fine gardens or wonderful countryside; the countryman, of fine cities made of gold. The poor imagined riches, fine raiment, all the food they needed and eternal rest. The rich found it more difficult: they were afraid of losing what they already had or of being punished for having it. Perhaps it was the rich who helped bring about the fear of death. Look about you, they still fear it to this day and are the ones who go in for cryogenics and methods of finding everlasting youth.

Some have always advocated the tenet of reincarnation. They do not consider what will happen to the soul immediately after death, preferring to pass it over by saying it sleeps until reborn or is at least unaware. Others have thought of the idea of sleeping until awakened, not to be reborn but resurrected in their last earthly body.

As these ideas formulated and gained strength, it caused them actually to happen just over the borders of death, just past the veil. Some of them are still there. Heavens of all kinds and conditions. Happy hunting grounds are on the wane but there are many others in full swing. Cities of gold and jewels, gardens with cool running water, etc. There are equally souls lying asleep, waiting for whatever it is for which they wait.

There are also the ideas of places of punishment for those who did what was thought to be wrong. All of these places can be found, and if any soul fervently believes that is what life after death consists of, that is what they will find. Not only find but be trapped within it. Their minds think it should be so and it is. When the 'joys' of any particular heaven begin to pall then they can be rescued from themselves and shown that there is so much more. This trapping of the soul is one of the worst aspects of the old dogmatic religions. It is growing less as religion is ousted, but now there are more drifting souls with which to contend, souls who didn't believe there was anything after death and still don't believe they are dead.

As I have said, there are many books in Spiritualistic literature that can acquaint you with the facts. A little research will uncover any number of books which describe all sorts and conditions of humans passing to the etheric realms. I will not go into details but try to show you how knowledge of the kind I have tried to provide you with in this book will be of assistance to modern mankind who, as I have just said, has quite often left behind these ancient ideas of heaven.

Let us first take the soul who has realised that it exists – the 'I exist' principle – but not awoken that spark of love and started to bring it forth. This soul may be at any of the many levels of its progression. If it is very deeply entrenched in the things of the earth life it has just left behind in death, it will stay in the realms close to the earth plane. Indeed it will almost interact with it. That is to say it will be observing the things that are happening on earth rather than anything in the etheric realms. It will hang around the areas that it knew and close to the people with whom it consorted. It may see other souls who are in a like condition and later drift off to areas that appear to be just like the earth it knew. It may even find souls that it once knew and who are similarly tied to a low level. This may be the first indication to the soul that something has happened, and that something is death. Where is the help I spoke of? Ah, that was an example of a soul that was slightly more progressed. At the level I am talking about I regret to say the soul will have not earned any help and so it will not be forthcoming.

This is not an easy thing to accept, for one likes to think that all loved ones will be all right in the next world. I cannot always assure you of this for, as I have said, here you are seen as you are, and what you are regulates where you can go and what help you can get. If you have not learnt anything about the nature of the soul, not even common decency, then unfortunately you must suffer the consequences. These souls may wander in dark drear conditions for many, many years.

Some won't even drift away from the environs of earth and will become very much entangled in the Astral layer, the layer which is slightly denser than the etheric but not as dense as the physical. It is the layer which helps the soul incarnate and leave the earthly body. As you leave your body you have a shell of the astral particles which, in most cases, soon vanish, leaving only etheric particles. But those wishing to affect the earth will cling on or even re-gather an astral shell if they have lost their own. It can be so strong that, given the right conditions, it can be seen by those still incarnate. Clairvoyants will see these souls very easily but even non-clairvoyant people can, at times, see them. This is what gives rise to stories of ghosts, poltergeists and so on. To the incarnate they are nothing that should be feared. Some will manifest with seemingly evil intentions while others appear to be lost or seeking something or someone. All should be dealt with in a firm manner. The lost and hopeless should be told they are dead – they often don't know – and to look about for those who can help them. This is often enough to make the soul open its mind and receive help. Souls of a more difficult nature may need experienced help, and I do not mean those who come with bell, book and candle and recite formal intonements. The poor souls who are lost will bolt in fear and still not be made reachable by those waiting in the etheric to help. Yes, someone is always waiting to help. The more malevolent will just laugh for they would have been unlikely to have thought much of religion and religious services while in the body. You see this type of soul is not ready to be helped and can only be told to go elsewhere. This they can do. There are mediums who undertake this sort of work but not all succeed and even those good at this work do not succeed every time. Negative forces can build up in a place until it would take one of the truly great masters to clear such a place.

Why do I talk of lost souls being in this dark place if I said their nature can be seen and that dictates the place to which they go? They may well have developed some attributes of the soul which will be noticeable but not the knowledge to go with it, which may not be their fault. They may hold some preconceived idea which also could be the reason for their presence there. For instance, it is from these lowly realms that the idea of purgatory comes, a place not quite heaven, nor yet hell. Nobody puts the soul in purgatory but some souls do find themselves there not so much because of lack of progression but because of lack of real knowledge. It has been noticed that people who have this tenet of purgatory in their religion do tend to land up there. That is because it is where they strongly believe they belong. Very few think they are good enough for heaven. Many of these souls are quickly helped, for they have earned that help and only lack knowledge.

As a place can be attractive to these lowly souls so can a person. An incarnate can attract a soul, but here the law of like attracting like operates. If you are not of a similar lowly quality to one of these souls it is doubtful that one of this kind will attach itself to you. But a caution must be given to those who begin to open the windows of their soul. They must take care never to let in the deceivers. This is why there are the warnings in the previous chapter and why it is wise to seek an experienced teacher. Always, always test the ideas and teaching you receive in meditation or inspirationally. If they are not of a quality that you would wish, discard them immediately and do not allow that source to manifest again. Ask for help, from the highest source that you can possibly conceive, to keep them away. If you have made a mistake and the teacher is genuine they will not mind; they would rather you doubt and were sensible enough to ask for help, which will come in abundance if sought.

Once the lost and misled have been found and rescued, they, like those who arrive in the etheric with just a little more knowledge and advancement, will be taken to the realms of light. It will seem pretty much like a pleasant earth and there, after recuperation, begins the long awakening. Because of the state into which the earth has fallen with dogmatic religions, lack of knowledge and long-standing greed, it is found that in most cases souls have little or no real idea of the true way life and death works. In between each incarnation they have to be re-taught, reminded of their past, their prior existences. Most souls, up until now, have not even been told as much as we have discussed in this book, for mankind has only just begun, generally, to be of an educational standard that they may be able to understand such things. Of course there have been souls who were of a higher standard, who had begun to understand a little in their earth lives, but most were not ready. After a period of time, differing in every case, the soul will return to earth to try again, for each is brought to the point where they realise it is only in the physical where they may find that which they seek.

Those in the dark regions also return to earth but without the benefit of tuition. They are souls who will undergo the natural tuition of Karma and will eventually come to learn.

If you have some knowledge whilst on earth and put it into practice – by that I mean alter your way of life to live in harmony with all things as much as possible – which will naturally mean you tend to do the right thing, then death is merely a short pause while you get your bearings and then you are on your way to delightful discoveries, sweet seeking and loving companionship. You too may later return for a further life on earth or you may decide or find you no longer need its rigours. For this to happen you must be at a particular standard of progression and this varies from person to person, for we are all different. What yours is only you can say. You may be wrong and this will be gently pointed out and you may have to change your view.

Whatever, it is the seeker who has the run of the etheric realms and the ever increasing joy as the soul rises into their higher reaches. Their possibilities are endless.

At any one time there are always those who are at the end of their earthly incarnations and who will begin to climb the levels of the etheric realms. There, as I have said, they will find their twin soul and experience all the joy of that reunion. They will learn and work until the time comes to pass out of the realms of earth and take form on the finer etheric universes and then onwards as explained elsewhere.

At any time you may have been having the joy of discovering the souls of your own soul-cell. This intensifies on the climb upwards and later is increased by the further happiness of reunion with the soul-cells of the total soul. You may well feel that it all seems reasonable up until the point that I start talking about merging one soul into another. It may still repel you. This is where falling in love in the earthly sense is the natural way to begin to feel the wish to be at one with another. Those in love wish they could pass their feeling directly into the mind of the loved one. No words are adequate. The physical act of love does not even suffice to express their feelings if they truly love another. They wish they could mingle their minds, take on each other's sufferings and woes. Although in some instances a very close relationship can occur and even have signs that thoughts can be transferred to each other, messages sent, it is not quite what is desired.

In the etheric and following spheres this is achievable. Not only once, in the follow-on of earthly loving, the twin soul's reunion, but again and again as the souls meet greater and greater loves. It is all a part of stimulating the love force within. It is only in the recombined form of the total soul that the individual soul can possibly bear the higher spheres and re-merge with the Great Spirit.

Do not worry too much about it but keep an open mind. When it is time for it to happen you will be in the state for it to happen and will wish for it to happen. Until then it cannot possibly happen. If, however, you are beginning to feel that you long to have a boon companion, that something is missing, that you would love to share with another totally, then you have begun to feel the pull of your soul-cell. I suggest that in moments of quiet you think of your soul-cell mates and, if there are any in the etheric, they will come to you or more, be drawn to you. It may not be until after death that they can make themselves known but it will make them more aware of you. If they are on earth at the same time as you they may well still be drawn to your company. Then you will recognise them by your feeling for them. Do not be surprised if they do not feel so much for you for they may not be of your standard of progression yet. But still there is usually a liking at least.

This drawing by thought is done by the message passing through the residual network of energy and etheric particles that composed the original soul-cell. This also connects with the total soul network of mind which still exists. It is this that is sometimes referred to as the over-self, the total-self. Some term it the group soul which is really nearer the mark. You are always a part of your group and can, should you wish, use the collected knowledge of the group. For you see, even as you exist now, the knowledge is passed through the network and absorbed by the total group mind. As you advance and rejoin your group so you learn to make use of this combined knowledge. This is one of the reasons for there being a group, as I have said before. It means each

individual or soul-cell does not have to do everything.
Between the whole group, though, nearly everything will
be covered.

In an earthly state you can put a problem to your group
mind and find the answer. Not always, for the answer
may not be known, not yet learnt. Then you must turn to
others for aid; maybe the soul that guides your complete
soul, or a little nearer, one who is your own particular
teacher or friend. Do learn to ask for help of any kind. It
sets in motion the thought form of seeking help. It is like
a flag out in the etheric which draws attention and
interest. But a warning: be careful for what you ask – that
it is worthy – you do not want to draw the wrong kind to
give the answer.

Now I wish to return to our symbol of the Spiritual
Universe for the last time. We have talked of going up and
down levels and this gives the idea of steps or going
higher or lower, going from one sphere to another by
stepping over the border. It is not really this way at all for
it is all a matter of dimensions. When one goes from one
to the next it is as if the last one fades out and a new one
fades in. You yourself do not move. How can this be? It is
because all dimensions exist by interpenetration and
therefore within each other.

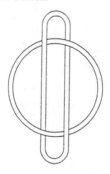

We have already taken the circle of our symbol and squashed it in sideways. Now we will take it top and bottom and squash it again. Do you see what happens? The circles had been drawn symbolically one above the other; even then this was not so for everything is in the same place at the same time. This is the thing to understand, that each dimension, each sphere is where all the others are. Hence the energy network of the Angelic sphere, the mind network of the pre-Angelic sphere and the source, the Great Spirit itself, all interpenetrate each other. This may be how the thought that 'God is everywhere' came to be. The Great Spirit is everywhere as are Its legions of souls as personified in the mind and energy states, even in the matter states, which is where we are.

There will come sometime to those that seek – it may be whilst in meditation or just when in an open state of mind, while in the physical or the etheric – that they feel as if they are about to understand the very nature of the universe, as if they could mix and mingle themselves with it and feel its total life. This comes in degrees according to the development of the soul and it is always very wonderful. It shows that the soul is near what some call enlightenment. They have brought themselves to the border of two dimensions, the latter is fading but still visible and the other about to materialise to the soul, for they have raised their level to that of the higher dimension. This can happen whilst on earth but it is very fleeting, for the physical soon brings the soul back. It has been known for the very highly advanced soul to die at that moment and actually go to the higher dimension. It is to this that Buddhists refer when they speak of enlightenment and reaching 'Nirvana'. It is by no means the ultimate but something that can happen to souls that have advanced themselves spiritually.

The seeker becomes the finder of the fuel, a most important moment in the life of any soul. The finder then has to become the transporter and 'a journeyman', that is one who has completed an apprenticeship and starts work for an employer. Work is the key to the journey home. We all work, and we are all the employers. We all put our knowledge to use. It is not that we have finished with learning, far from it, We study harder than ever, but now for a higher purpose. We have our interests and hobbies, much as you on earth. We have our pleasures and rest times. We have our times of fellowship with friends and intimate interludes with loved ones. We also have our times of failure and regret, heart-ache and even loss. But the difference is that we either know or are shown how to cope with problems and sort them out. Here, once in the realms of light, there is an abundance of help, help from more advanced souls whose work it is to help just such as us. We, in our turn, try to help any whom we can, or assist in projects directed by others. Be sure you will find something to interest you and give congenial companionship and many hours of occupation.

The difference between your work and ours is that yours is to earn a living. We no longer have this to drive us on. In fact it is having to work on earth that teaches the soul how to work. We can all be naturally lazy. What we call work here is done for the benefit of others in almost every case. We enjoy the labour and are gratified if it is of use. Very few truly enjoy their occupation on earth. Here one's occupation is enjoyed and if not completely enjoyed is known to be of value, worthwhile and appreciated. Our occupation will also change from time to time as we learn and we may even lead a team on some project if we are the right one to do so. One may easily be the leader one day and less than the dust the next because of lack of knowledge on any particular subject.

The important thing is that we are very busy: our life is not limited to drifting around and endless sloth. Does the earth teach one sloth? Not for most people. So taking our law of gradual change, preparation for the next stage, you must begin to realise that the physical earth is also a training ground for the lives etheric. You have learnt to control a body, learnt what it is like to have a body. You have learnt ethics and behaviour, how to conduct yourself, you have learnt how to study and apply that study in work and play. Most of all, you have learnt about your inner being and how to express it, you have learnt to love. All this is why you have lived on earth, why you are now living there. All this is why you must not waste one second in useless, harmful and wasteful pursuits. All this is why you must never consider terminating your life prematurely, for no matter how hard or painful your problem, there is something which you can learn from it. It may even be exactly what you came to learn this time.

Learning is the reason for your present existence, learning and trying out what you have already learnt, seeing if you remember your lessons. In life you learn the things of existence, of being; in seeking you learn the things of the soul and find the fuel of the Spiritual Universe. That is the reason why you have life. Enjoy it and be sure the fuel you bring home will be of the very best quality. Your journey home will refine and shine that fuel until it is perfect and used in the continuance of not only every other soul but your own soul as well.

Chapter 14

Light on some Perplexities

Where, you might ask, does prayer come into all of this? We have spoken of meditation, finding the inner self, but not of addressing ourself to or through anyone. Quite so. I did mention the kind of prayer that was a cry from the heart of a soul. I have not spoken of formalised ritual prayers. Let us think about it in the light of what we have been discussing.

It is tied up with thought, mind and the stages leading to the Great Spirit. I have tried to explain that thought is a reality beyond your world, a living reality. What is prayer if not a thought? It is the quality of that thought that matters in what mankind terms 'prayer'.

Now the cry from the soul, that moment, that split second when a fervent wish, hope, longing, need, leaves the mind of anyone, is what I mean by a cry from the soul. If you could watch it from this side of life you would see something like an arrow of light pierce through the gloom and shoot towards its target. It goes to whomever it was addressed to directly. It could be addressed to one of the Holy Spirits, such as the Buddha or Jesus. They are actual souls who lived on earth and therefore, of course, exist in the Universe. If it was addressed to a mythical god then it is received by a Spirit who is interested in the particular area of the world from which the cry arose and who may be the spirit on whom the idea of the god was originally formed. If it is addressed directly to whatever the person's idea of God is, then it will go to the Christ Spirit. It is rare for any to address the Great Spirit directly for it has been understood by so few that it existed. As I have said, mankind was only just about able to conceive the Christ Spirit as God.

For an answer to be given to this arrow of prayer, it is necessary that the receiver is capable of answering it. For instance, many souls who are termed 'Saints' by the Roman Catholic church receive such prayers. Often they are unable to make an answer themselves and they take it to one whom they think might be able to help. It will be a soul of greater knowledge and wisdom than themselves. This passing on may continue until it reaches the Christ Spirit. Even then the Christ Spirit may pass it to the Great Spirit Itself. Such an aimed prayer is always received and equally always answered. The trouble is that we do not always recognise the answer. It rarely is the answer for which we asked. But it will be the one that is suitable to our needs and those needs may be tempered by the application of Karmic forces.

Fine, but what about formalised prayer, mantras and so on? To be quite straight with you, the majority are a waste of time. Sometimes they can help to concentrate the mind before meditation, settle one down, lead the thoughts in the right direction. But mostly they hardly even rise an inch above the speaker before falling apart into dust.

What about all the hours and hours that some ecclesiastics spend in prayer? The countless services, orders of worship so carefully thought out? The droning of Buddhist monks, the turning of prayer wheels? The dutiful prayers of the faithful Moslems every day? All those grand words written and spoken, hymned and sung over thousands of years? *Have they all been useless?* Regretfully, and if you knew my own personal story you would understand my own regret, regretfully I must tell that yes, most of them have been absolutely useless, the reason being that there was no real effort put into them, no effort of mind, no thought form as in the case of the arrow of the heartfelt cry. They were not really meant. Not only that, many of them were not even needed! There is a thought for you.

The concept of 'worship' must be called into question, lauding, giving praise. For what does a spirit that is absolute in Itself, is everything, need with praise? It does not need to be told It is marvellous, wonderful, because It is those things even if It is never told them. It does not need to be told them for purposes of boosting its ego. Having been told them, or if they have been withheld, will make not the slightest difference to the being of the Great Spirit. So why do we continue to do it? Pour out millions of words telling the Great Spirit, or our conception of God, how marvellous, wonderful and good It is?

The answer lies deep in human history. If you make a study of man's growing understanding of his spirituality and his relationship to his changing idea of what God is, then it is easy to see that man could only think that God thinks and acts like a human, a human who was at the top of the hierarchy, the very top. Now most people's experience of those at the top was that they held the reins and when they said jump, you jumped, or it was the worse for you. You obeyed them, feared them. To get what you wanted you had to make your top person happy and you did that by a combination of fawning, flattery and abasement of self. Most of all you gave gifts. They had to be gifts that outdid your rival's gifts. If you pleased your lord and master, you dared to ask him for a favour. If you annoyed him by going against his will, you hid from his wrath.

With your idea of a god being a superior lord and master your approach to it would be very similar. You would laud it up to the skies, tell it how clever it was and how humble you were. You would offer gifts of worth, a practice later encouraged by priests who make good use of those gifts, and if everything was going awry for you, you would suppose that you had done something wrong, something to annoy the god and it was showing its wrath. On planet earth it does appear that things seem to go horribly wrong more often than be pleasant, so the gods often appear to be very angry and vengeful.

I am talking nonsense about these ideas of God? Really? You take the time to study the words addressed to 'God' so glibly year in and year out. They follow exactly the pattern I have just outlined. To my mind, in the light of my knowledge, they are an insult to either the Christ Spirit or the Great Spirit.

About the only exception I could make in this plethora of unneeded verbiage is in being thankful, grateful. For thankfulness is a form of love. It leaves the heart of any soul wrapped in a warm feeling that is truly real and meant. It has form. Even then, if you watch a priest intoning prayers among which was an expression of thanks, you would see that it rose no further than any other of his useless words. But that moment of thanks – when your life or the life of a loved one is not lost, or a child is born to you, or it is a lovely day and you just feel everything is so good you could shout for joy – that prayer, those thanks travel up through the spheres delighting everyone whom they pass on their way to the very heart of creation.

Neither the Christ Spirit nor the Great Spirit need any forms of worship to continue to love and care for all. They will go on doing it, asked or not. Nor do they get cross at anything we do or do not do, saddened I am sure they are, but not cross and therefore not wrathful or vengeful. Loving they always are. So mankind must begin to act as the advanced modern homo sapiens that he considers himself to be and put aside the ideas of his childhood, grasp new concepts of what God is all about. It is time to do away with what was really a prop to himself in a life of continual worry and fear of the horrors that planet earth could mete out. God will not be found in that manner. God, the Great Spirit, will be found within yourself. There you will find that you are the Great Spirit. It is yourself that you address should you essay into formal prayer. How obviously stupid. And why should you 'fear' yourself? All things pass and are replaced by the new. Formal worship must be seen for what it is: a useless exercise. It should be replaced by a true exercise of the soul and is why I recommend the soul to search within and without by study and meditation. This can be done separately and in groups.

A further burden often laid on mankind by theologians is that they are told they must seek to do 'God's will'. This must surely be seen to be a ploy to keep the people in

check, keep them firmly held down. The only 'will' is
yours and mine and everyone of us individually. It is a
will that is entirely free.

Nothing is ordained that it will be, but plans can be
laid, expectations can be hoped for, if it is the will of all the
people, the souls who can bring any particular thing to
pass. You were given free will, or rather you were left
untrammelled by any other will being forced upon you, as
soon as you left the Great Spirit. You continue to have that
freedom to choose and will always do so. It is only with
that freedom that you can wander the Spiritual Universe
on your journey with the unlimited ability to find
somewhere, in the welter of your experiences, that
priceless jewel, your individual discovery of love and a
way of expressing it.

What we do all have is a purpose. What the Great Spirit
did ask of us was to go out on a quest, a holy quest if you
like, a quest of that which is needed. So there is a purpose
to our existence, a reason why we are. That you enjoy any
part of that quest is a bonus. That you suffer in any of it is
unfortunate but necessary. It is the sacrifice you made for
all souls and the one they make for you. Without their
sacrifice you will not continue to exist nor they without
yours. For each brings back from its journey its findings,
its knowledge, which will be just that little bit different
from every other. Within that knowledge will be found the
jewel. This jewel is a symbol for something which is very
hard to express in language. It is an individual way of
looking at love, an individual way of giving, expressing
love, using love, how that is used within the source that is
the Great Spirit we do not know.

If you think about it, the Great Spirit is a blank to us.
We do not even consider the idea of anything going on

within the source except maybe some 'thinking'. We just imagine it as being 'The Source of all Things', the activity on the outside – manifested – and tranquillity, stillness within – unmanifested. I wonder? I wonder if we have got even that wrong? If it was stillness and tranquillity, nothing disturbed, why do we struggle so hard to learn about activity, fight to bring that hard-wrung knowledge back home? Perhaps because inwardly we know that it is where it will truly be of use. Our efforts appreciated. Perhaps there, we will find the greatest activity of all.

It is so far beyond us all, this concept of the Great Spirit and our reunion with it. We have not even grasped the concept of our own Logos, that spirit who is the same as us yet so different, the Logos that is of the Great Spirit and is the Great Spirit, as are all of us, yet different in that it is near perfect; perfect in the respect that it has travelled out and back from the source so many times that it has a total knowledge of the Spiritual Universe, a total ability to use it, manipulate it, set in motion the possibility of a complete new Universe. But remember it is not done totally alone. To the Logos' positive was sent out the equal negative that I termed the Diablo Spirit, the light and the dark; the principle of two throughout all things.

I have not talked much about this side of the nature of the Great Spirit. Let's face it, it is not a side that is likely to be attractive to mankind in trying to get them to open their minds. Terror and fear have been attached to the dark side of things for thousands of years. There has only been one slightly loveable characteristic given to the personifications of this spirit, a rather rascally, fun-loving nature, more mischievous than evil, likely to play tricks on people. One has a slight admiration for an old rascal, other than that it is Machiavellian all the way, deceiving and down-right evil.

I would put the Diablo Spirit as more of a brooding nature, a depressive nature, the negative propensity to resent. When it sends personifications of itself – which is to say spirits who are its close followers having incarnations, as is the rule – they are not all negative and so the positive comes through, often as this rather loveable rascally nature. For you see 'love' is still the basis of their particle of the source just as much as the positive souls. All that happens is that the negative nature hides it, buries it, smothers it. This is true of the Diablo Spirit itself; another way of saying negative souls are souls that have taken the wrong turning, the wrong road and landed themselves in a lot of bother. Yet I put this to you. Who knows that it is not the negative within all of us that actually brings about the finding of the jewel? It causes the suffering which seems necessary, particularly in our universe, to find ourselves, our inner self. Without it we would go home empty-handed or at least have to search for a far greater length of time. The search is long enough now!

So the negative force of the Diablo Spirit affects the negative in all of us, however large or small that part of us happens to be. Equally the Christ Spirit affects the positive in us, the two causing the tension necessary to bring the reality of our situation into focus. In a way it is a catalyst of situations that might lead us to find knowledge of interest, gain experience or even find our own soul and therefore the fuel we seek. How dull life would be without that tension.

The tension can manifest in something as small as a little frustration to a downright battle, or a mild pleasure of being with good companions to the joy of doing a tremendously good deed. The battle may be a simple confrontation between neighbours or be as vast and terrible as a world war. Of course there are all the shades in between that make up the history of your planet, the history of the etheric realms and finer etheric worlds, in fact the whole of the Etheric/Physical Universe. For the Christ Spirit and the Diablo Spirit affect them all. They do not just pertain to your small planet. What does pertain to you are the souls, the Holy Spirits and the followers of the Diablo Spirit, who manifest on planet earth, and who incarnate there.

We have mentioned this before but I would like to consider it a bit closer. These spirits have come to earth from time to time under what might be called the direction of the force to which they adhere. They would have left the Great Spirit at the same or about the same time as the ancient single total souls and have been attendant upon them throughout the Pre and Angelic spheres. That is to say they would have been companion total souls. They would have ranged from souls who might only break down into two soul-cells and no further to relatively large numbered souls who break down into individual souls. How many direct followers each force has is not known for, in a way, we all can be their followers and used, should we wish, in any situation that may arise. For having formed the Etheric/ Physical Universe, the two Spirits become immersed in it, almost personify as it and remain in constant tension that it may continue. A balance has to be continually found and maintained. Should one side or the other become over-dominant it could mean the end of the universe. Now I have said this universe of ours is predominantly negative. That is its balance just as you have a balance between the two in you. This means that if the balance slips towards the negative it makes things very bleak indeed. For this negative manifests as the black side of life, the uncomfortable, the disruptive, the evil element which causes so much harm.

It is rather like a person being depressed. It brings out all the gloom and despondency in their nature. During the depression they may do things that are harmful to others and to themselves. These days this is quite often understood and taken into consideration when dealing with the misconduct of some people. The opposite is elation, a raising of the feelings of happiness and joy. During such times a person will be happiness and light to all they meet. They may even take upon themselves some travail or hard job of work, accepting its difficulties with great joy.

The two forces in our universe work in this way; they are an influence. It does seem possible that those of great stature can actually deal directly with these spirits, these grand total souls, and receive instructions of how to proceed. But for most, and especially for us, it is an influence. For both are beyond our real conception.

In the way the Great Spirit sets out the Christ Spirit to be our idea of God, the Christ Spirit sets out his Holy Spirits to bring things down to our level. It asks souls of varying stature to journey down into matter and personify as a human-type on some physical world. There are many sent, each to bring that comprehensible form to any planet where souls are at the level of, or equal to homo sapiens, including homo sapiens. They will appear throughout the history of those worlds and, as in previous states of existence, they never pass without being noticed. They are subject to all the laws of the universe, just as we are; they have no ability to suspend those laws, but what they do have is greater knowledge and experience of how to use, manipulate those laws, to the point that to ordinary souls, it does seem they have extraordinary abilities, supernatural powers. *THEY HAVE NOT,* never forget that. They are abilities that are available to anyone who knows how to use them and are still a part of this universe's laws.

Those spirits that I term the Holy Spirits and pertain to our Christ Spirit are not hard to find within our history. As I said before, they do not all start new religions, they just show the way by the example of their own lives. They will of course show the positive side of their nature more profoundly than most. Those who come on behalf of the Diablo Spirit equally profess the negative. These souls too, can found new ways of thought and be leaders of exceptional quality, have magnetic personalities that draw people to them. Or they may just be those disruptive and unpleasant persons we all meet from time to time. Examples of these negative souls are not hard to find either and one came this century, one of the most negative. He brought with him a whole host of like minds and at the same time others were attracted to incarnate in different parts of the world. Between them they nearly brought the planet earth to its knees. It was a concentrated effort to pervert and destroy planet earth before it reached its new age, the new age of knowledge of self.

The Christ Spirit had to put out an equal force to combat this stream of evil that came at that time. You may think the battle ended many years ago between the two forces but it did not; it has continued both on your earth and in the etheric and still continues to this day. But with a final effort we can right the balance of your planet and make it a tenable place to have an incarnation, a place with just the right amount of tension for souls to learn, the kind of advanced souls that will make up the new age.

It is a mistake to think all will be happiness and light and that discomfort will be a thing of the past once the balance is restored. It will not, for that has never been the purpose of your world, or rather the use that has been made of your world. It is a place of discomfort, of easy corruption. It will not be any different in the future, but with knowledge of how to use it properly comes the chance of a better life for all. Those there in that future age will still die, despite their efforts to avert this 'dread' happening. They will learn to postpone death but it will never be conquered. For if souls stayed on earth forever they would not be fulfilling their purpose, which is to return home with their joyful burden of fuel. The wish for eternal earth life is a negative wish, a diminishing of the wish to show love by taking on the toil of the homeward journey. Whereas those at the point of wishing to get on their way almost long for death. It is one of the signs that they are ready to move onward.

It is found that positive souls who appear to show goodness and light are more easily understood than the negative. It can be understood how they find the love source within themselves and bring it through, for their whole nature leads them to it more easily. To understand how a negative soul loses its undesirable qualities is more difficult. Well, not all negative qualities are evil; it is rather that they can only be turned to evil use more easily.

Every trait in character can be looked at two ways. Tolerance to one is allowing domination to another. Stubbornness in one is tenacity in another. Greed in one may be gathering the wherewithal to help others. Think of great charity fund-raisers. The list is endless, and you can think up more examples. Many positive traits can be used for evil purposes. Leadership is a great positive quality to have, yet can lead to domination for evil purposes. And so a trait may be turned and used for good or evil purposes but it is usually in the good purposes that a new way is found of looking at love. Yes, it all leads back to the same thing for positive or negative, which are words that I have to use for lack of any other to express a concept. Both, both are part of the whole. We are all one. We are all on the same journey and together we will, in our turn, refuel the Spiritual Universe, each in our own way, each using the forces of soul, be they positive or negative in almost totality or a balance of the two.

We have mentioned that there has been a personification of the negative force this century, though not by name. It is not necessary to reinforce his infamy by mentioning his name. But there is one of the positive forces' personifications that must be spoken about for he was a Holy Spirit incarnate of great magnitude. He came after many others had come to earth and tried to show mankind how to keep the balance right on this earth. The others came at various times and to various peoples of the world. None have ever been left without a soul to help them, a soul of great light.

Two thousand years ago, or thereabouts, came one so great that his fame now encompasses the whole of your world. I do not mean that he has displaced the other Holy Spirits' ideas and teachings, but even if his ideas were not accepted as suitable for any particular region of earth, he is still known about and mostly respected. Of course that one is the Jew called Jesus, later called 'The Christ', the Anointed One. That even later it became a suffix name – almost a family name, a surname – is odd, but the interesting fact is that this man showed so much of the Christ Spirit in his nature that the name was appended to him in the first place. And so he is now called Jesus Christ and is looked on as the Christ Spirit Itself.

Although this is incorrect it is not entirely wrong in the fact that it was as a guide to understanding the Christ Spirit that he came to earth. He was someone to whom the peoples of earth could relate their ideas of God. As they grew out of the conceptions of the gods or God that early man had envisaged, they needed a new concept and he came to give them just that, lead them towards what he called the 'The Father' which is the Christ Spirit, God as we imagined it. He succeeded admirably and is responsible for mankind moving forward in its concepts of spirituality. But this was two thousand years ago; its original form is now very thinly spread upon the ground and adulterated with the many attentions of the followers of the Diablo Spirit. Yes, of course, that force tried to pervert it right from the start. The positive force did everything possible to maintain its purity of message but it nevertheless became tarnished and remoulded to suit the passing ages.

Today you are left with a mish-mash of ideas about this man ranging from the consideration of him as a god in his own right – as early men made gods of men – to his being merely one more messenger of God. The truth is somewhere in between. If God, or what we thought of as God, the Christ Spirit, came to incarnate on earth, I feel It would have been much as Jesus was. So Jesus does give us a very good idea of the possibilities of God, the love of God. But if the Christ Spirit is not God but a personification of the Great Spirit, then certainly the soul who incarnated as the man, Jesus, is equally not God but a personification of the Christ Spirit, that which man has always thought of as God.

Jesus was a messenger of that God, of that there is no doubt. But the message today is adulterated and confused. It is also outmoded for modern day man. Outmoded, you note, not outdated, which implies that it was wrong and new ideas must supersede it. The actual teachings he gave are as relevant today as they were in that tiny land two thousand years ago. But the trouble is to know in the welter of superimposed 'teachings' what his actual teachings were. I know, for I can consult true records written by the man himself. I can try to tell you but why should you believe me, a discarnate man writing through an incarnate woman. You would say either it was the woman herself and her ideas or that my ideas were coloured by her. You certainly would be right in the latter instance.

It is not important that I tell you which they were. What is important is that you re-find those truths for yourself for that is what the new age will be all about. It will not be an age where you take another's word for these things. So you will no longer have to take the word of such people as the medium or me, the man who lived so long ago and who brought a way of showing the truths of the universe to suit the people of that time, and those for many years to come, those leading right up to your own time of greater intelligence and the dawning of a new age.

It begs the question, will one come to lead the way for the new age? The medium stops typing on her machine for she fears putting down an absolute to such a question. She does not want to be in the position of being called a prophet. For you would look at her so. I would be putting information through her mind which could change it. This could be applied to anything in this book and it seems to be side stepping an issue that would be provable one way or the other. So let us look at the question in another way.

I have been telling you that you 'are God', that the

Great Spirit which is the name I give God is the Flame of Life, the soul within each and every one of you. You yourself can turn inwards to find this and I have tried to show you this in my explanations. Should you care to do so, you may turn inwards and find the answers to questions such as this one, or at least your own helpers, friends of the spirit will help you find an answer. If you think it is an important question then you must search diligently for the answer. Whether one comes or not they can do no more than reiterate what has already been said a million times. I am doing no more than that, merely rephrasing it in modern language. This is why it is not important what, or who, you think I am or am not, it is what is written here that is important and the use you make of it.

I personally respect and love the soul who personified as Jesus, as I do the other wonderful Holy Spirits of the Christ Spirit. He still is a leader among leaders and remains within the environs of the etheric realms of Earth, for he is our particular personification of the Christ Spirit to whom we can all relate. It is through knowing him that I came to know of the Christ Spirit and began better to feel its power and love force. It will be through the Christ Spirit that I am pointed towards knowing and finally rejoining and being the Great Spirit. All is one. I cannot say this often enough. We follow a wonderful chain, a rope of pearls of great quality, each bettering the last in its lustre and perfection until we find one so wonderful we cannot express its beauty and perfection, only let go and merge with it.

It is possible that another personification of the Christ Spirit will come to your earth for an incarnation. It has been done before and it could be done again. Indeed, as I have said, there are personifications on earth at this moment though not of the stature, of course, of Jesus, or even some other great souls. You have your modern facilities to hear news of the whole world. These souls come to be noticed as all great souls are noticed and their doings reported. If you use the way of looking at the world that I hope I have imparted to you, you will find them for yourselves.

Find them and wonder, for they personify in their lives what you must seek to personify. Do not worry that they do it so much better than you, that is their God-given responsibility. You personify the love source to the best of your ability and you will be loved as much as the greatest soul that ever was by the Great Spirit, for I must repeat, you are as important as any other soul and without you we do not continue to exist. We have our being in one another, at whatever level of understanding and progression of the soul we are at, from those just starting the journey to those near its end and those who at this moment make up the source, the wondrous heart of the Spiritual Universe, the Great Spirit, the Ultimate.

Yes even the Great Spirit Itself is one of us. It is like a trillion, trillion multi-souls merged to become as one. It works on the same principle as ourselves. Perhaps, to be more correct, one should say we work on the same principle as the Great Spirit for – *ALL IS ONE.*

Unless you seek and find the fuel, learn how to transport it home, the Great Spirit cannot continue to exist. This is the task with which we were charged and one that we must carry out for our very own existence to continue. Many worry about being blotted out, ceasing to be. The only way this can happen is if you and I and all souls did not carry out our task. That is a near impossibility but not totally so. Without *YOU* there would be a piece missing from the pattern; it would be incomplete and it could fall apart, collapse, cease to function, for the least is as important as the greatest in this pattern of life in the Spiritual Universe where *ALL ARE ONE.*

THE END

Appendix

Since writing this book I have been asked to speak about it at various meetings and groups of a 'spiritual awareness' nature. With the comments of those that have read the draft of the book added to the questions raised at the lectures, I feel that there are a few points I would like to make that might help to make sense of what is an enormous subject. I feel that some symbolic diagrams plus a few more words may clarify what Alpha is trying to tell us.

When the book was written I had not really read much about atomic or cosmic structure. Indeed I had read very few books on psychic or spiritual matters either. Most of my learning was from this internal source I call Alpha.

During the last five years I have felt as if I was released from a bond that did not allow me to read such books. Perhaps it had been a good thing for my mind was fairly clear of other people's ideas and so this book was able to get through with new ideas. Now I have caught up with my reading and what do I find? First of all Alpha is in agreement with many spiritual teachings, new and old.

Secondly, his cosmic structure fits in with many of the newest ideas in the world of science put forward by Hawkins, Seymour, Sheldrake and Schilling, to name but a few. But Alpha's message is so much wider, goes so much further. He is not limiting our understanding to what is cosmically very near to home. He is saying we must wake up and take our place in the greater whole. I hear so much about human 'leaps of consciousness and spirituality'. Yet the questions I am asked most are often limited to our present incarnated state and maybe just through to the next. Important as this is we must now try to lift ourselves above this rather selfish stage and progress to larger views – or fail utterly to do the work we came to do in this particular part of the whole Spiritual Universe.

*   *   *   *   *

The most important points in this book are

1. The far wider aspect of the experiences of the Soul than just worldly incarnations.
2. The idea that our conceptions of 'God' have been sadly limited.
3. That everything is all part of one whole being, manifested and unmanifested.
4. That this Being is evolving and changing by our efforts while voyaging on the Journey of the Soul.
5. That this Being has to be refuelled and that is the reason why we, you, I and every other soul in any other form, leave the centre of all Being and go on the Journey of the Soul. If we didn't, that Being – our own Being – could cease to exist!

Which is the most important of these points? Undoubtedly the last. It gives the answer that we all seek to the 'What am I doing here?' question. I have lived with this idea for thirty years and it has saved my reason many times, made sense of what appear to be stupid and unreasonable happenings and given me hope. I hope it does the same for others.

One of the things that seems difficult to understand is Alpha's 'group souls'. The 'Total Soul', when leaving the Great Spirit to start its round of externalised existence, is rather like a seedcase that is unripened and held tightly closed. All the seeds are within different segments of the whole seed case.

In this state they experience the mind or pre-Angelic realms and the energy or Angelic realms. When they enter the Etheric/Physical Universe the seedcase has ripened and is bursting apart into its segments – 'Soul Cells'.

In this state it experiences the finer etheric worlds and then the heavier etheric steps down to a physical world. During this time the seed segments ripen and it bursts apart again.

The seeds – the 'Individual Soul' – are now free to experience separate incarnations in the physical and heavy etherics. You could say they are 'planted' into the heavier worlds to grow and blossom.

One could take holograms as another way of looking at it. If you cut a piece from a hologramatic picture it has the complete picture still within the piece. As the total soul breaks down into soul-cells, they all take with them a smaller part but with everything still there. The same happens again when the soul-cell breaks down and the individual souls take an even smaller part which still has the whole memory of everything the complete total soul and soul-cell has ever experienced.

Beyond that, in actuality, all individual soul-cell members are still joined by threads of what might be termed energy. Equally all soul-cells are still joined together in the same way within their total soul. You have these threads that join you to your groups right now! These other souls and other soul-cells are more than your family, more than just loved ones – they are YOU!

Another way that Alpha has helped me to understand it is by taking me on a mental, or meditational journey, back to the source. But calling it a 'journey' makes one think of going from place to place, here to there. It is not this at all but more a fading out of one dimension into another. We are all used to this concept in science fictional films. Rather as in 'time travel', the machine stays in the same place with the time traveller on board. The present fades out and the age, forward or backward, is faded in.

Here is a meditation which you can try. I suggest you record it on a tape and then play it whilst meditating. Find a quiet, comfortable place where you will not be disturbed and relax. If you have a separate player, you could put on some unobtrusive music for the duration of the meditation.

Alpha's Meditation
Instructions in brackets not to be spoken
Feel your physical body, its weight upon the chair. Know you are safe and that if you wish you can ask for a guide to accompany you on this experience. You can return at any time that you wish just by opening your eyes and feeling wide awake, happy and relaxed.

Close your eyes and take some deep relaxing breaths. Let go of the physical reality in your mind and become conscious of your etheric body. It is much lighter in weight, it seems almost to float.

(ALLOW SHORT PAUSE BEFORE NEXT WORDS)

After you have experienced this for a while be conscious of even lighter bodies as each layer of heavier etherics are left behind. Eventually you are in the lightest of your etheric bodies and ready to let go of even that. During this you may be conscious of changing scenery or just a feeling that the light gets brighter and brighter.

(ALLOW SHORT PAUSE BEFORE NEXT WORDS)

Now you let go of the etheric altogether and feel yourself to be energy. You experience the feelings and sensations of this energy, its colours and forms.

(ALLOW SHORT PAUSE BEFORE NEXT WORDS)

But this too gets lighter and lighter until you leave this behind and move into pure mind. Quiet, peaceful, beautiful mind. This feeling expands you until it too is left behind and you find yourself expressed only as love.

(ALLOW SHORT PAUSE BEFORE NEXT WORDS)

Stay still and listen. Here you are face to face with the Great Spirit using that part of you that is the Great Spirit, your central flame of life. Listen and you may hear that which is right for you to know at this time.

(ALLOW LONGER PAUSE BEFORE NEXT WORDS)

When ready, feel yourself being drawn back SLOWLY through the dimensions. In each you regain its particles and see the realms through which you pass as you personify in each. Gradually, gradually,

Mind   – (PAUSE)
Energy   – (PAUSE)
Finer Etherics – (PAUSE)
Deeper Etherics – (PAUSE)

until you can again sense the physical body and you return to your present incarnation bringing with you the memories of your experience. Take some deep breaths and when you are ready open your eyes.